BEST HOME HINTS
FROM THE SUPER HANDYMAN

Best Home Hints

FROM THE SUPER HANDYMAN AL CARRELL

TAYLOR PUBLISHING COMPANY, DALLAS, TEXAS

Book design by David Timmons Graphic Design
Illustrations by Boardwork, Inc.
Copyright © 1990 by Al Carrell

Published by Taylor Publishing Company
          1550 West Mockingbird Lane
          Dallas, Texas 75235

Library of Congress Cataloging-in-Publication Data
Carrell, Al.
          Best home hints from the super handyman / Al Carrell.
                    p.   cm.
          ISBN 0-87833-753-9 : $12.95
          1. Dwellings — Maintenance and repair — Amateurs' manuals.
2. Do-it-yourself work.
  I. Title.
  TH4817.3.C36 1990
  643' .7—dc20   90-35324
                                                      CIP

Printed in the United States of America
10 9 8 7 6 5 4 3 2 1

To the four women in my life:
Jean, Kelly, Meg, and Sarah

Contents

A WORD ABOUT SAFETY

Nothing compares to the satisfaction a completed home project gives you. And the most important ingredient in any do-it-yourself job is safety-consciousness. I can't stress enough the importance of knowing your tools, your products, and yourself when working around the home. Check and doublecheck your equipment. Read product labels carefully. Invest in safety goggles, tough work gloves, sturdy clothes, and a hard hat. Keep a first-aid kit handy in your utility room, workshop, or car. Make sure your children understand what tools and work areas are off-limits to them. And, most importantly, have a safety-first attitude.

I have marked with symbols those hints in this book that require safety-consciousness. These symbols indicate when you need to wear safety goggles, when you need to wear a face mask, when materials are flammable, when skin protection measures are necessary, when electrical shock is to be guarded against, when materials are poisonous, and when ventilation is crucial. Watch for these symbols and, in the spirit of the Boy Scouts, be prepared! Your do-it-yourself job will be both successful and safe.

 Goggles

 Flammable

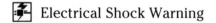 Electrical Shock Warning

 Poisonous

Ventilation

Mask

Skin Protection Needed

The Basics:
Tools, Materials,
The Workshop

TOOLING UP

The Basics

Even though many of the hints in this book will let you in on tricky ways on how to accomplish a chore with a substitute tool, the better way is to have the tool meant for the job. This doesn't mean that you'll need a bunch of state-of-the-art, laser-driven, twenty-first-century omni gadgets. It just means that you'll need a few fairly inexpensive basic tools. Here is the basic list:

- **Hammer** – Get a carpenter's claw hammer. Don't get one that's too light in weight. The sixteen-ounce size is a good choice. Take a few practice swings before you make your choice.
- **Screwdrivers** – Buy a set containing a variety of both regular (slotted) and Phillips-type screwdrivers.
- **Pliers** – You'll find a medium sized slip-joint pair to be useful.
- **Saw** – A cross-cut saw will also cut with the grain.
- **Wrenches** – A ten-inch adjustable type will take the place of several wrenches.
- **Electric drill** – This is the most basic of power tools. Go for a $^3/_8$-inch model that is a variable speed and is reversible.
- **Utility knife** – for safety, select one that has a retractable blade. Keep a supply of extra blades.
- **Stapler** – Get one a little more hefty than the type used in the office. The models that can handle several sizes of staples are handier.
- **Level** – A pocket size is adequate. A longer one is better.
- **Measuring device** – Retractable tape types are inexpensive and easy to use.

- **Flashlight** – Check it from time to time to be sure it's working.
- **Fasteners** – Your dealer will have assortment packs of nails, screws, nuts, and bolts.
- **Tapes** – A roll each of electrical and masking tape will hold lots of things together.
- **Lubricants** – Machine oil and a spray lube are enough to start.
- **Glue** – White glue won't do it all but helps many times.
- **Plumber's friend** – Get a plunger that's big enough to cover the kitchen sink drain opening and your ready to fight most clogs.

Tool Box Tips

Broom handle

Crowbar is handle for toolbox

Once you have your collection, it's a good idea to keep it all together in a tool box.

Make your own tool box

You can make your own tool box out of an old cabinet drawer. Make a handle for it by installing a broom stick between the center of the front and back of the drawer, up near the top.

Or, if the drawer is deep enough, drill holes to accommodate a crowbar as a handle.

Tuck it in a bucket!

If you don't want a proper tool box, maybe a plastic bucket will do. You'll find use for the bucket after you get a real tool box.

It's in the can!

Join four coffee cans together using small nuts and bolts. Make a handle from a section of plastic clothes line or rope. It'll carry lots of tools and materials.

Double Duty

Make a wooden box with high ends to which you add a 2x4 as the handle. This doubles as a mini sawhorse, which can be very handy.

Coffee can tote

Cut a rug!

Cut a carpet scrap to fit in the bottom of the toolbox. It's kinder on the tools and quieter, too.

Cut the rust
Put a cone of carpenter's chalk inside to absorb moisture. A few mothballs will do the same.

April showers!
Make a raincoat for your tool box by cutting a slit in the bottom of a plastic bag to fit over the handle. Trim off the excess plastic that hangs below the box.

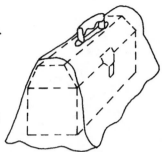

Bottom of trash bag is raincoat for toolbox

HANDY TOOL TIPS

Buckets

Holey buckets!
Here's a bucket tip. If it develops a leak, you can pinpoint the leak with an extension cord and light under the up-side-down bucket.

Once the hole is spotted, you can drip candle wax over it on the inside of the bucket. You can now use it again, but only for cold water.

Or, use a hot glue gun that will make a permanent patch.

You can also line the inside of the bucket with a sheet of plastic that drapes over the rim.

Hammers

A new hammer
Scuff sand the face of a new hammer to prevent glancing blows.

Soften the blows
A rubber crutch tip, also called a furniture leg tip, can be slipped over the face of a hammer to convert it into a mallet to prevent damage to the work surface.

Or, crisscross a couple of adhesive bandage strips over the face.

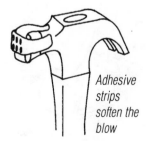

Adhesive strips soften the blow

Making a mallet
Shorten the handle of a croquet mallet and glue leather on one face and you've got it!

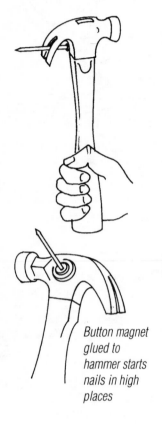

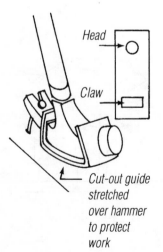

Replacing a handle

Put a new hammer handle in the oven for a while to remove moisture from the wood. Then shape it and, when it's installed, moisture from the air will cause it to expand for a tighter fit.

Just before inserting a new handle into a hammer, coat the top with epoxy glue. It's set for life!

Too loose

A loose hammer handle can be put in a container with linseed oil for an hour. The oil causes the wood to swell for a tighter fit.

Extra reach

When starting a nail that is too high to reach, wedge a nail into the "V" of the claw. It will hold well enough for the first couple of taps. Then let it go, and you can drive it home.

Instant attraction

Here's an idea you'll be drawn to. Glue a button magnet to the side of the hammer to hold the nail in high places for those starting taps.

Button magnet glued to hammer starts nails in high places

Clever clawing

When extracting nails with a claw hammer, a rubber, wedge-shaped doorstop acts as a fulcrum for extra leverage and also protects the work.

A flat pencil eraser can also help.
Or, make a cover from a scrap of an old inner tube as shown.
How about a magazine?
Or, try a plate scraper from the kitchen.
A wide rubber band pulled over the face and claw to form a figure eight protects the work.
Or, slap an adhesive bandage strip over the claw.

Leftover scraps of peel-and-stick weatherstripping can be glued to the hammer top to prevent marring the surface.

Sometimes the nail wedges in the "V" and won't fall out. A tiny dot of silicone sealant in the "V" prevents this.

Head

Claw

Cut-out guide stretched over hammer to protect work

Keep it quiet!

When hammering inside the house, deaden some of the noise by hammering on the phone book. Good for apartment living.

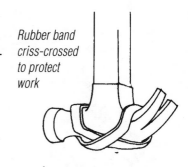

Rubber band criss-crossed to protect work

The quick pick-up

Glue a button-type magnet to the bottom of the handle. When you poke this into your apron pocket, you'll draw back a small supply of nails.

A holster

Tie a large roll of masking tape to your belt as a handy hammer holster.

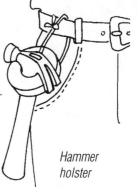

Hammer holster

Nailset

Easy to find

Install a slip-on pencil clip on the nailset and keep it in your shirt pocket.

Since this tool is always used with a hammer, use a rubber band to hold the two together.

Screwdrivers

Picking the right one

Use a solder gun to burn a "-" or a "+" in the top end of screwdriver handles. The "-" is for slotted and the "+" is for Phillips. Now, if they're stored with the handles up, you can easily pick out the type you need.

Pencil clip on nailset

Get a grip on it!

Glue a rubber bike handlebar grip over the screwdriver handle for a better grip.

Mark slotted and Phillips screwdrivers

Hold on

Dig the blade into a cone of carpenter's chalk. The chalk gives the screwdriver better holding power in the slot.

Or, put some scouring powder on the tip for the same result. Powder power!

A few strokes in the grooves with a triangular file will restore the bite to a Phillips screwdriver.

A tab of masking tape pulled over a blade that's loose in the slot solves the problem.

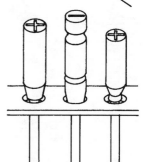

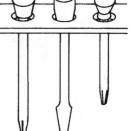

For greater turning power, use a screwdriver with a square shaft and grip this with an adjustable wrench.

With a round shank, let the wrench grip the tool on the flat tip.

Which way?

Don't know which way to turn? For screws and most other things, remember: "Right is tight!" or "Clockwise is lockwise!"

A handy mini-tool

Make a tiny screwdriver by filing the end of a sardine can key.

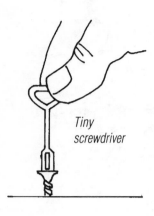

Tiny screwdriver

Saws

Tooth tips

Apply a coat of paste wax to saw blades. It protects the metal and lets the saw move through the work more easily.

Or, use a candle stub.

When sharpening your saw blade, run the flame of a candle back and forth along the teeth, leaving a trail of soot. This way you can tell at a glance which teeth have been filed.

Or, cover the teeth with a liquid shoe polish . . . or a felt marker.

A slit length of old garden hose over saw teeth protects the tool in storage.

Aluminum foil dipped in kerosene will clean resin deposits from the saw blade. 🔥

Or, use paint thinner in a spray bottle. 🔥

Severe gummy deposits can be removed with oven cleaner.

Prevent this problem to begin with by sawing through a bar of soap before you start sawing the wood.

As a rule . . .

Use an electric etching pencil to make inch marks on the back of the blade to have a handy ruler.

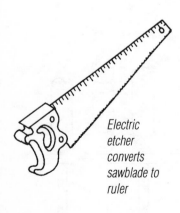

Electric etcher converts sawblade to ruler

Hacksaws

Best tooth forward
The teeth on a hacksaw blade always face away from the handle.

Cut-ups
Need a wider cut? Place two or more blades in the hacksaw frame.

If the hacksaw frame is in the way, wrap tape around one end of a blade to use as a handle and use the blade by itself.

A broken piece of hacksaw blade can be gripped by a C-clamp to become a keyhole saw with a handle.

If there isn't room to saw a pipe, remember that the blade can be installed upside down in the hacksaw frame over the pipe.

A good way to store extra blades is to tape them to the top of the hacksaw frame.

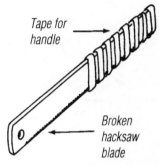

Tape for handle

Broken hacksaw blade

Saw business
A pair of plastic spines used in business to hold reports and presentations together will easily slip over a saw blade to protect the teeth.

Pliers

Open wide
Slip a short length of old garden hose on the ends of plier handles. You have a better grip, and the jaws open automatically.

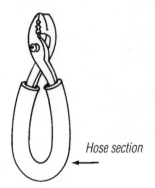

Hose section

Don't bite
Cut a couple of fingers from an old leather glove to slip over the jaws of pliers to protect your work surface from teeth marks.

Double duty
Use a grinder to shape one of the handle ends like a screwdriver. It won't be worth much as a screwdriver but can do some handy prying.

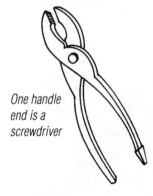

One handle end is a screwdriver

Wrenches

Gain without pain
Push against the wrench with an open palm. If there's a slip, you won't smash your knuckles.

Re-cycle grips
Give your small adjustable wrench a better grip by slipping a bicycle handlebar grip over the handle.

Bike handle grip

Pipe dream
A small pipe section slipped over the handle of an adjustable wrench will add to the length for extra leverage . . . but not so much that you break the tool.

When you have a stubborn task for an adjustable wrench, remember that the fixed jaw is stronger than the movable jaw, so push your force toward this strength.

Wrench cinch
To corral the sockets in a wrench set, find a nut to fit each socket and glue them in a line in a tool tray. The sockets stand on the nuts until needed.

A big safety pin like those used in laundries will hold an entire set of box wrenches and hang from the shop wall.

Both sockets and box wrenches can be kept together on a long beaded chain.

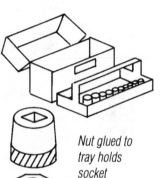

Nut glued to tray holds socket

Files

Clean teeth
Remove filings from the teeth by pressing masking tape firmly into the file. When you peel the tape up sharply, the filings stick to the tape and come out.

Or, use a brass-bristled suede shoe brush.

Handy Handles
For a file without a handle, poke the tang (pointed end) into the rubber tread from an old bike pedal. It gives you a good grip that's easy on the hands.

Or, use the same trick with a sponge rubber ball.

Fill a spent shotgun shell with epoxy glue or two-part pouring resin. Then insert the file into the wet mixture.

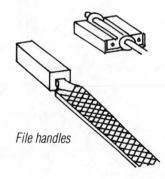

File handles

Be sure it's held in place while the epoxy hardens.

PVC plastic pipe with a pipe cap can be used the same way.

The old-fashioned door knob with a set screw to hold it in place can also become a useful file handle.

Resin-filled PVC pipe handle

En garde!

When sharpening a blade, protect your hand by putting a large metal washer over the tang.

Sharpening Stones

Stone cold clean [6]

Soak a whetstone in kerosene to clean.

Or, boil it in water for ten minutes.

Place it in the oven. The heat will melt the oil, and it will carry out filings as well.

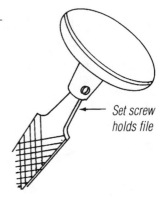

← *Set screw holds file*

Stone storage   [6]

A sardine can is ideal for some sizes of stones. Use a foil cover and add a little kerosene.

Or, wrap it in foil, pouring in some kerosene before sealing.

Or, store it in a sealable plastic bag.

A plastic storage tub will also work well.

Utility Knife

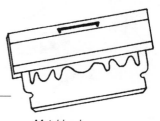

Matchbook cover makes blade safe

Looking sharp

A few swipes across the striking surface of a matchbook cover will keep the blade sharp.

Moisten the edge of a clay pot and use it to sharpen.

Or, use a step on an aluminum ladder the same way.

Razor blades

If you use this tool as a substitute for the utility knife, use the single-edged variety. If you use a double-edge blade, tear off all but the striking surface of a matchbook and let that slip over the blade as a handle to protect your fingers.

Carry a razor blade inside a matchbook.

Or, inside an aspirin tin.

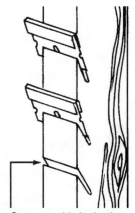

Store razor blades in slots

In the shop, make slots in a wall stud slanting down to hold them.

Or, use a scrap block of rigid foam packing material.

Chisels

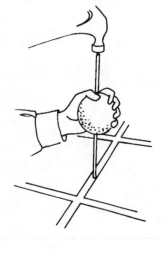

Handling a chiseler
If using a cold chisel or star drill, poke a hole in a sponge rubber ball and push the ball to the center of the shaft. The ball acts as a shock absorber from the hammer blows on the tool.

Locking grip pliers can also become a dandy handle.

Flying rocks
Of course, when using a chisel to break concrete, you should always wear your safety goggles. As a way to contain some of the flying concrete, poke a hole in the center of a piece of screen wire and put the chisel through the hole.

Or, put the chisel through the bristles of a broom. This trick also holds the chisel in place so your hand is away from the action.

For small jobs, let a plastic coffee can lid act as a shield.

Or, if you have a plunger that no longer creates much suction, drill a hole through the socket where the handle goes. With the chisel through there, the cup plays catcher.

The Plane Truth

Just plain smooth
Warm the sole with a hair dryer and then rub a candle stub over it. The coating will let the plane glide better.

Sock it away
An old sweat sock is great for storing planes.

What did I miss?
Draw a squiggly line along where you're going to plane. This will let you know if you've missed a spot.

The Vise Squad

A base hit
If you'll install your vise so the fixed jaw sticks out over the edge of the bench, you can hold work vertically as well as horizontally.

Pinch proofing
The vise handle can't pinch your hand if you use a large rubber band with a slip knot around each end. The handle still moves but can't accidentally slide and play "gotcha."

Just looping rubber bands around each end will give the ends bumpers so you don't get pinched.

Avoid teeth marks
When holding finished work, protect it by using a sheet of old inner tube between the jaws and the work.

Or, glue carpet scraps to the jaws.

Plastic coffee can lids or kitchen sponges can also protect work.

Or, use a pair of rubber heels from shoes.

No pipe dream
A discarded leather belt can be wrapped around a pipe. The vise can grip the tails of the belt as close as possible to the pipe and hold the pipe tightly.

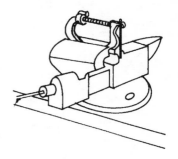

The mini vise
If the vise is too big for the work, put a C-clamp in the vise. The vise holds the clamp and the clamp holds the work.

An even smaller vise can be had by using a screw-on earring.

Or, use a pair of tweezers held tightly and closed with a small C-clamp.

Clamps

Take the bit out of clamping
A small crutch tip can be used on a C-clamp to protect the work.

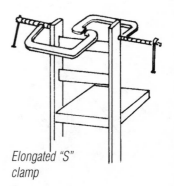

Elongated "S" clamp

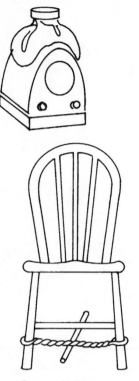

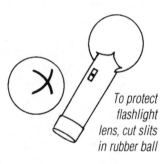

Rope and stick act as clamp for glue

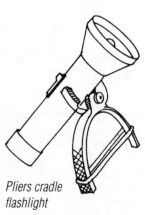

To protect flashlight lens, cut slits in rubber ball

Pliers cradle flashlight

Clamp camps

C-clamps can be stored by clamping them to the edge of open shelves.

Or, clamp them up the legs of the workbench.

Alternate clamping

If you need a slightly larger C-clamp, use two. Put the face of each clamp together and you'll have a sort of elongated "S" clamp with a longer reach.

Often your clamping pressure is accomplished with just heavy weights. Books or bricks can be carried a few at a time and you can end up with as much weight as you need.

Rather than carry the weights, why not fill containers with water from a hose after they're in place?

For irregular objects, fill a plastic bag or an icebag with sand and shape it over the work. The weight will hold it in place.

For big flat work where you need weight, place it on the garage floor, cover the work with scrap plywood, and then drive your car over it for weight.

Bands cut from an old inner tube will pull parts together for gluing.

Or, use a rope and a stick to twist the rope tight like a tourniquet.

An old nylon stocking can be stretched out, twisted tightly, and used just like the rope.

The Light Touch

Flashlight flashes

To protect a flashlight kept in a tool box, make two slits to form an "X" in a hollow rubber ball. Stick the lens end of the flashlight in and it's protected.

Use a magnetic flashlight and attach it to the side of your tool box.

Attach a C-clamp to the bottom of the flashlight to act as a base which will hold the light at any angle without falling over.

When working in a crawl space, you can stick a pair of plier handles in the ground with the jaws open to cradle the flashlight.

Or, attach the flashlight to a tire iron with a rubber

band. The sharp end can be jammed into the ground and the light adjusted to where it's needed.

Drop-light props

Add a wooden drawer-pull to the metal shell so you can adjust the light without burning your fingers.

Install a spool on the wall with a nail that sticks out from it. Coil the cord around the spool and hang the light by its hook on the nail.

Loop the cord and tape it to the handle so there's no stress on the cord.

Make tape loops at the plug end so unplugging puts no strain at that point.

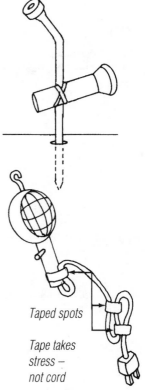

Step Ladders

Safer stepping

Give all ladders a visual inspection before every use.

A screen door hook and eye will prevent the ladder from coming open in transit.

Install a metal towel bar toward the rear of the top step and you have a hand rail to steady yourself.

Or, attach a large C-clamp to the top step.

Ladder adders

Install a screen door handle in the center of a side rail for one-hand carrying.

Drill a few holes of various sizes into the top step as a place to store hand tools while not in use.

One of those metal toothbrush and glass holders from the bathroom wall can be attached to the side of a ladder. The glass holder can keep a container of fasteners, and small tools go in the brush slots.

A wall-type broom holder will hold a hammer on the side of the ladder.

Use Velcro to hold small tools on a ladder.

Frame the top step with a small molding so that small parts can't roll off.

Glue small magnets around the edge of the top step to help corral small parts and tools.

Or, run a bead of caulk around the edge to keep parts in place.

For a bigger top step that will not let anything roll off,

Taped spots

Tape takes stress – not cord

Metal towel bar as hand hold

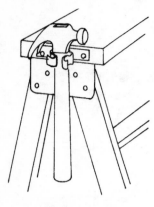

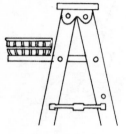

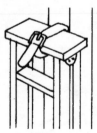

Leather belt holds
ladder to wall

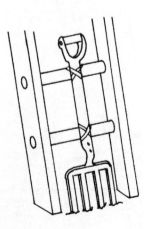

just clamp a TV tray on when needed.

A wire bike basket on the fold-out paint shelf will hold lots of tools and materials.

Install a small, L-shaped angle brace under the bottom step and on the inside rail to use as a foot scraper. Cleaner shoes mean surer footing.

No footprints

To prevent the ladder from marking up the floor as you move it, make four shoes from the bottom of waxed milk cartons.

Storage

A ladder that's left against the garage wall when not being used is liable to fall and dent your car. Attach an old leather belt to the wall so it wraps around the top step and buckles.

Or, use a screen door spring and hooks to hold it.

If you live in an apartment and there's no place to store your step ladder, put houseplants on each step and put your "plant stand" in a corner until it needs to become a ladder again.

Straight Ladders

Ladder landings

A sandbag against each rail will prevent the ladder from sliding out from under you.

Poke a garden fork into the ground and tie the ladder to it.

Put each leg into the opening in a concrete block to keep the ladder in place.

On soft ground, stay on top of things by clamping a 2x4 across the ladder at the bottom of the legs.

Those old overshoes will look funny on your ladder but will prevent slipping on a hard, smooth surface.

No mark-ups

Slip work gloves over the top ends of the rails to protect whatever the ladder will lean against.

Or, wrap with carpet scraps, using rubber bands to hold the pads.

Cleaner climbing
Cover the bottom rung of a ladder with burlap to wipe feet for better grip as you climb.

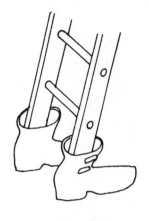

Handy holding helpers
When working on a ladder, keep a wide rubber band around your thigh to hold small tools.

Straighten a wire coat hanger and then make a slip knot of it around a rung with the hook part aimed down as a bucket holder.

Unsafe ladders should be taken out of service. Attach the side rail of the ladder to the shop wall and you'll have some nice bins in which to store lumber. Angle the ladder and you'll have bins for different lengths of material.

This is not a rung number
An aluminum ladder with hollow rungs offers an opportunity on your next paint job. Push a broom handle through the rung with several inches sticking out on one side. Cut a notch in the handle and it will hold your paint bucket right at your side.

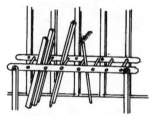

Ladder attached to shop wall becomes rack for materials

Storage
Hang the ladder horizontally from heavy-duty, L-shaped shelf brackets. To be sure it can't fall off, hook a screen door spring from the wall to a hole in the end of the bracket.

Security
Never leave a ladder stored outside or a thief may use it to climb in a second-story window. If you have to leave one out, chain it to a tree.

Sawhorses

Handy horse holders
Add a shelf under the sawhorse and you have a place for tools and small items.

Cut four side pieces and this shelf becomes a bin for your tools.

Use a short section of guttering plus two end caps and you have a nice tray for the side of the horse. Put one on each side.

Saddle bags for your sawhorse

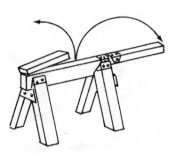

Fold-out arms give sawhorse wider support

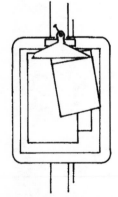

Clipboard hung on workshop wall helps keep sandpaper straight and handy

Use peg board on the ends of the sawhorse to brace the legs and you'll also have a way to hang the tools being used.

Install cans on the end of the top rail of the sawhorse to hold small tools.

Or, staple the bottom halves of plastic jugs to the sides. It's like having saddlebags.

The soft touch

Pad the top rail with carpet scraps for less chance of scratching the work.

Measure up

Glue a yardstick to the top rail for quick measurements.

A winged horse?

Attach a pair of hinged wings to the center rail. When folded out, the sawhorse can better handle 4x8 sheets of plywood.

Tall in the saddle

Make a removable piggyback piece for a sawhorse. Cut a 2x4 to the same length as the top rail. Install four metal mending plates so they'll fit over the top rail and hold the piggyback in place.

Sawhorse subs

A good substitute sawhorse can be made using a pair of two-foot ladders with a 2x4 clamped in place. Use a 2x12 and you have a short scaffold. And the ladders have other ladder uses too.

If you are an apartment dweller and have no sawhorses, use a pair of open back breakfast chairs with a 2x4 resting on the seats.

Abrasives

Storage

A record album cover is number one on the hit parade as a place to store loose sheets of sandpaper. Mark the grits on a tape on the front of the jacket.

Use a clipboard as a holder for loose sheets of sandpaper. The clip holds the sandpaper and the clipboard hangs from the wall.

The sands of time

Sandpaper will often last longer if you'll tape strips of masking tape across the back.

Sanding savvy

Wrap sandpaper around a hacksaw blade to get down into a narrow slit.

Deck of cards with sandpaper

Wrap sandpaper around a deck of cards and press against a curved piece. The cards will conform to the shape. A tight grip will keep the shape to get the sanding done.

For very small items, put the sanding block in a vise and move the workpiece back and forth.

An emory board makes a nice mini-sander for many small tasks.

Door-stops as handles for sanding block

If you'd like a two-handed sander, install a screw-in type door stop in each side of a 2x4 and sand away.

New, unwrapped soap bars can be handy sanding blocks and come in several sizes.

A worn shoe brush makes a good sanding block for irregular surfaces. Hold the abrasive in place with rubber bands.

Wrap a strip of sandpaper around a spoon and hold it in place with your forefinger. It's good for sanding curved spots.

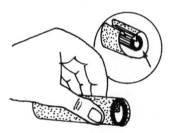

For sanding inside curves, you can make a sanding block from a short slit piece of old garden hose. Cut the sandpaper to fit with the edges inside the slit.

Clean sanding belts by holding an old crepe shoe sole against the moving belt.

Curved sanding block

For sanding up high, let a sponge mop give you a hand. Remove the sponge and wrap the sandpaper around it. When the sponge is put back on, the frame will hold the sandpaper, and you've got the extra reach.

Steel wool

To avoid splinters of steel wool, hold it with half a hollow rubber ball.

A butt hinge holds steel wool better than your hands, too.

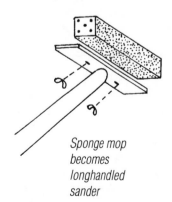

Sponge mop becomes longhandled sander

Or, poke it into a spent shotgun shell.

Clean away all the slivers by running a magnet over the work.

Adhesives

Spread the news
Use the end of the tube of glue as a spreader.

An old car wiper blade is a good glue spreader for wide areas.

Your old pocket comb spreads glue well.

Or, use a sawtooth cutter from a box of wax paper.

A stronger bond
Sprinkle fibers from a filter-tip cigarette into the glue.

Or, add a few strands of steel wool.

Ready...set...glue
Drill holes in a shelf to store glue bottles upside down. The glue is in the spout, so you won't have to wait forever until the stuff oozes out.

Tidy tricks
Mask along each edge of wood to be glued. Then, when clamping squeezes out the glue, clean up is easier.

Put wax paper under glue projects so the project doesn't end up stuck to the work table . . . or the clamps.

Mix small amounts of epoxy on aluminum foil. When the job is done, toss the messy foil.

Or, put both components in a zip-up plastic bag. Mix by kneading the bag. To use, turn the bag inside out. When through, turn the mess back inside and can it.

Gluing those hard-to-reach spots
A hypodermic needle is great for shooting glue down into narrow surfaces.

Sticky subs
Make your own glue by burning off the solvent from shellac. Pour the amount you need into a fireproof container and ignite. The remainder is good for gluing wood, glass, and other materials.

Or, use fingernail polish.

Sticky situations
Two-component epoxy is activated when you mix. If you mix up the caps on the tubes, you have probably glued them both in place.

With any glue, the cap can get glued in place. This won't happen if you smear a little petroleum jelly over the threads before recapping.

After placing the cap on the glue, wrap it with foil so it's air tight and you'll never end up with a tube of dried-up glue.

Glue clues

Before gluing bare wood, use a hair dryer to heat and dry the wood to be glued. This removes moisture and opens the pores to accept more glue. In the case of a chair rung, the wood will shrink and then after it's glued it will expand for a tighter fit.

Tapes

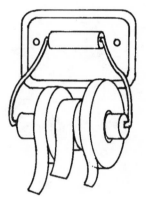

An indispensable dispenser
One of those metal toilet-paper holders can be mounted on the shop wall and will hold five or six rolls of tape.

A stud of an idea
With exposed studs, drill holes in adjacent studs to hold a section of broom handle, or dowel, which will hold and dispense tapes.

In the bag
If you store seldom-used tapes in zip-up sandwich bags, they're less likely to dry out or pick up dirt.

Tape recovery
Dried-up masking tape will revive after about thirty seconds in the microwave.

POWER TOOL TIPS

Drills and Bits

The key to success
If you tape the chuck key near the plug end of the drill cord, the tool has to be unplugged to put new attachments in the drill. Since there can be no accidental starts, it's safer and you'll always know where the chuck key is.

Or, use a 1"x3" strip of old inner tube with slits in

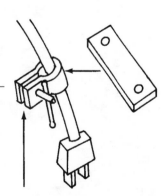

Chuck key held on cord with rubber strip

each end. Wrap this around the cord and force the small end of the chuck key through the slits.

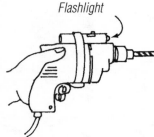
Flashlight

How deep?
When drilling to a specific depth, you can run tape around the bit several times and have a good depth gauge.

Lighten up
Often you need more light where drilling. Use a rubber band to attach a pen light to the top of the drill. The light is exactly where needed.

Fan-fare
Turn the drill bit into a fan that will blow away the dust it creates. Cut a strip of rigid plastic and make slits in the center for the bit to go through. As the bit turns, the strip acts as a fan.

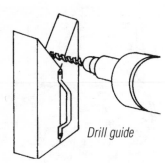

Drill guide

The drill on drilling
When you need to drill pilot holes for nails, snip off the nail head and put it in the chuck. You have a bit the exact size.

To be certain your bit goes into the exact spot, make a "V" notch in a 2x4 and add a screen door handle; the bit in the "V" can't stray.

In the buff
To buff ornate pieces, put a cotton swab in the chuck.

Good medicine
The proper size plastic pill bottle will fit over a drill chuck to protect it.

No-spill drill
Put a rubber band around a leg and run the cord from the power tool you're using under the band. Now if you trip over the cord, you won't be as likely to cause the tool to fall.

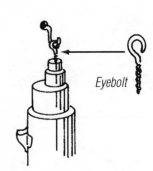

Eyebolt

Storage
Chuck an eyebolt into the drill, hand tighten, and you can hang the tool from a hook.

An old lunch box can be converted to hold a drill and bits.

Replace the lens of an empty flashlight with a tin or plastic lid cut to fit and you have a dandy bit holder.

A snap-lid glasses case will store a good variety of small drill bits.

Extra long drill bits can be stored in containers made from plastic pipe and end caps.

A bit cleaner [6]
Pour lacquer thinner into a skinny olive bottle and soak a dirty bit in this.

Circular Saws and Blades

Blade storage [image]
Store circular saw blades in old record jacket covers.

Protect the teeth with a large band cut from an old inner tube.

Use a pair of those giveaway shower caps from hotels to wrap the blade.

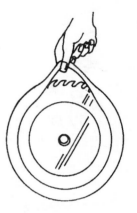

A cleaner blade [image]
An aluminum pizza pan makes a good soaker tray for round saw blades. If it's only slightly bigger than the blade, you'll require less solvent.

Smoothing the way [image]
Paste wax will protect the metal from rust and let the work move across a saw table with greater ease.

Sprinkle talcum powder on the saw table for less drag as work goes through.

Sawing safety [image]
If your table saw has a key, keep it on a safety pin attached to the band on your goggles. That way, you'll not easily forget the goggles when you get ready to use the tool.

Always use a push stick to run work through a table saw. A rubber plate scraper with a square notch cut out for the work is a nice, thin push stick.

Put a slip-on pencil eraser on a dowel to use as a push stick.

So your push stick doesn't get lost, use a string to tie it to the saw.

Never use a metal rule around a table saw. If it ever comes in contact with the moving blade, it becomes a dangerous missile.

Keep a plastic squeeze bottle around to blow dust away. When you use your breath, you often get some dust in your eyes.

A free saw table

A discarded washing machine can become a sturdy stand for a tablesaw. Leave the motor in for ballast. If it's a front loader, you might also add storage shelves.

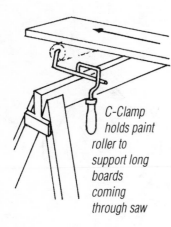

A fine fence

One of those magnetic bars made for holding cutlery will hold onto a metal saw table and become a good fence to guide the work against.

Rolling along

When running long stock through a table saw, use a paint roller clamped in place on a ladder to support the work.

C-Clamp holds paint roller to support long boards coming through saw

Bench Grinder

Squeaky clean wheels

Remove grinding wheels when they become clogged and put them in boiling water for fifteen minutes to clean.

For safety's sake

Hang a pair of safety goggles on the tool so you never start it without this protection.

When not in place, keep a wide band cut from an inner tube around the wire brush wheels to protect your hands.

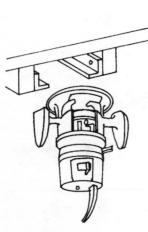

Router

A rack for the router

To make a holder that stores your router upside down, attach 2x2 lumber pieces to the underside of a shelf or cabinet. Then attach angle iron sections to the lumber pieces.

Router goes into slot

Belt Sanders

Storage ⌂
Install dowels in studs to hang sanding belts from.

OTHER TOOLS

Propane Torch

Got a light?
An old butane lighter that sparks but won't light can be used to ignite the torch.

Here's a matchless idea. Use a rubber band to hold a matchbook to the propane cylinder. You can strike a match while the matchbook is in place. Close cover before striking.

If a cold torch is hard to light, cover the air holes with your hand until lit.

Torch turn-off
You should turn off the torch when you set it down, but if you make a tip-proof holder you don't have to. Mount a large juice can to a two-inch thick block of wood.

Storage
Tie a loop of strong cord to the flame control knob and hang the torch from a hook on the wall.

Torch-toting tips
Add a handy handle to the cylinder with a screen door handle and a pair of worm-gear clamps.

Torch taters
If your hobby is jewelry making, stick the small parts into a potato when you're soldering. Use four nails as legs for the potato.

Torch touches
Start the barbecue grill with a torch to the charcoal.

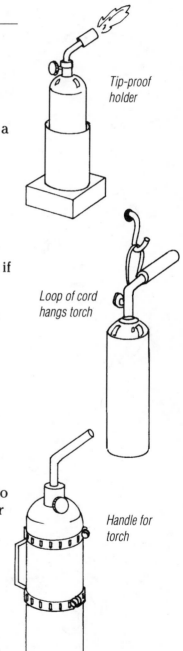

Tip-proof holder

Loop of cord hangs torch

Handle for torch

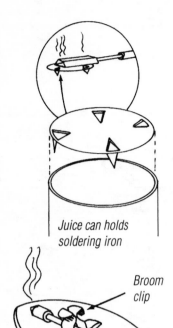

*Juice can holds
soldering iron*

Staplers

Finger savers

Use a thimble to bend the ends of staples down when the stapler doesn't complete the job.

Or, try the back of a spoon or a coin.

Foot savers

When you have a bunch of staples to remove, use a magnetized screwdriver to hold the staples as they're taken out. Otherwise, you will probably step on the one you dropped.

*Broom
clip*

*Bent can
cradles
hot solder
iron*

Solder Guns and Irons

A hot-plate

Using a punch-type can opener, punch four V-shaped holes in the bottom of a large juice can. Then use a regular can opener to remove this piece and you have a holder with four legs for a hot solder iron.

Or, press a sole plate from an iron into service. Attach a broom clip and the solder iron is held in place.

Crush an aluminum can to form a sort of V-shaped cradle that will hold a hot iron up off the surface.

Extra solder supply

Wrap several inches of solder wire around the electric cord to your solder gun in case your spool runs out.

Lighten up

Wrap solder wire around a flashlight and it's like having three hands when your soldering needs more light.

Another extra hand tip

When soldering wires, put two slit sections of garden hose in a vise. With the wires in the slits, both hands are free for holding solder and iron.

A branding iron

*Wrap extra solder around
gun cord*

Make a brand by fashioning a design of your initials from #10 copper wire. The ends of the wire go into the solder iron instead of a regular tip. When hot, put your brand in wooden tool handles.

Marking and Measuring Tools

The old carpenter's adage
"Measure once and you may cut twice. Measure twice and you'll only cut once."

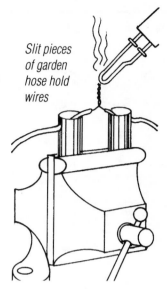

Slit pieces of garden hose hold wires

Can't read the numbers?
The stamped markings on framing squares, metal rules, and other tools can get pretty faint. Correction fluid from the office can be brushed on and then wiped off the surface, leaving the white stuff in the markings for better visibility.

A white crayon will also help.

Keeping track trick
A rubber band around a yard stick will act as a sliding marker to keep the place on the rule that you have measured.

Get your pencil ready
Wrap an adhesive bandage strip around your pencil with the sticky ends together forming a flap. Now the pencil can't roll off.

Stick a tack in the pencil eraser and glue a magnet under the bench top. The pencil will always be there.

A plastic pencil sharpener glued to the end of a metal rule is handy.

Glue one on the workbench, too.

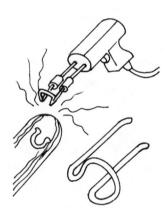

Make a brand from #10 copper wire

Where did I put those notes?
If you'll put a strip of masking tape on your arm, you can make note of all measurements and not wonder where they are.

Spend big to save a free yardstick
Tape a penny to the side of a razor blade to prevent slicing a wooden yardstick.

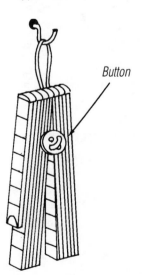

Button

As a rule
Wipe the blade of your retractable rule with waxed paper to lubricate.

A string loop with a button attached can become a hanging holder for a zigzag folding rule. Place the button against the center and run the string back through the

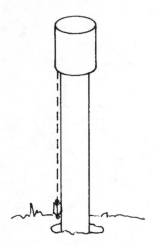

sections and hang the loop from a hook.

Plumb clever tricks

In the wind, a plumb bob can move. Put a bucket of water down and let the weight go into the water. It will stabilize and you can get the job done right.

A plumb bob must hang free to be able to tell if something is plumb. On a fence post, you need to bring the string away from the top of the post. Punch a small hole in a large juice can and hang the tool from there. The weight is free to give you an accurate reading.

Make you own plumb bob by tying a nail set on the end of a string.

Bubble trouble

Protect your level by putting a wide band made from a bike tire inner tube around the bubble vials.

Going around in circles

Make a giant compass for drawing circles from a strip of pegboard containing a line of holes. Drive a nail through a hole on one end and stick a pencil in one at the other and spin for a circle.

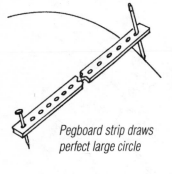

Pegboard strip draws perfect large circle

Miter Boxes

It's wired!

Use wire solder to follow a contour so that you can duplicate the shape.

A steadier miter

Add a section of angle iron to the bottom of a wooden miter box and it can then be held in a vise.

A handy rule

A ruler marking made in the bottom of your miter box will come in handy.

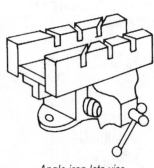

Angle iron lets vise hold miter box

A slick trick

Drip candle wax into the slits for easier sawing.

MATERIAL THINGS

Lumber

Storing lumber
Never store lumber on the ground. Old auto tires make a good storage rack for lumber.

Knots to you
Knots that fall out of boards can often be glued back in place with wood glue.

Hauling
When hauling lumber or even 4x8 sheets of plywood or sheetrock, place a couple of inflated inner tubes on the car top to tie the load down on top of them. No damage to the car.

Or, take out the floor mats and let them protect the car's roof.

Quick count
For quick measuring of lumber, mark off every six inches on the floor of your garage or shop. Start at a wall and you can slide the lumber against it.

Framing
Toenailing is the method of installing studs in a wall. The stud is put in place and nails are driven in at an angle to fasten them to the plates. The problem is that the hammer force of driving in the nails will move the stud out of position. Put a 2x4 spacer against the previous stud and then angle the nails into the other side of the next stud. The spacer holds the stud in place.

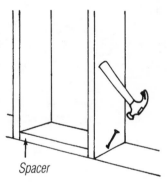

Spacer

Toe-nailing aid

Or, place a nail head against the stud and tap until the head is imbedded in the plate. When you drive nails in the other side, the stud cannot be moved.

Place the nail between two blocks to tap enough to curve the nail slightly. Curved nails toenail better.

Do away with toenailing by securing a 2x4 block onto the plate. Then drive nails through the stud into the block. A strong connection without toenailing.

Make your own "stop" when toe-nailing

Recycling old lumber
When reclaiming old lumber, fill nail holes with wooden

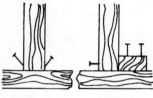

Toe-nailing   No toe-nailing

toothpicks dipped into wood glue. When the glue sets up, cut the toothpicks off with a razor blade.

Larger holes may need wooden matches.

Or, make a wood filler by mixing sawdust from the old wood into thinned nail polish.

Go over old lumber with a magnetic stud finder to spot any hidden nails.

Instead of trying to drive nails back out of old molding, just snip off the nail points sticking out. This is kinder to the wood.

When trimming off just a tad from a board, clamp a scrap over the work so it sticks out beyond the end by several inches. Now cut through both.

Wallboard

Moving it in place

L-braces convert skateboard into materials carrier

Sheetrock, or gypsum board, a very common wallboard, as well as plywood, comes in 4x8 sheets. The size and weight may make carrying a piece a bit uncomfortable. A metal towel bar extends your reach, and the hook on one end of the bar holds the bottom of the 4x8 sheet, while the top rests under your arm. Your other hand is free.

Or, use a crowbar the same way.

Rig a skateboard with four L-shaped brackets (as shown) to let you roll these big sheets to where they are needed.

There's also a rope trick for this purpose. Use an eighteen-foot piece of rope, joined to form a circle. Stand the sheet upright and loop the rope around the two bottom corners. Pull up on the center of the loop and the carrying is a snap.

Plywood

Making the cut

Place a sheet of plywood down on the lawn and, with the circular saw blade set to just the thickness of the sheet, you have overall support as you crawl across while cutting.

Prevent binding

When sawing a big sheet of plywood, about halfway through you may experience binding. Drop a nail into the sawed slot and it won't bind.

Metal

Cutting metal 🔒

Score the line to be cut with an old glass cutter which easily follows the straightedge. The scored line is easier to see and easier to follow.

When sawing metal, run the saw blade through a candle stub first and metal dust won't clog the teeth.

If you'll be cutting with tin snips or shears, rub the intended cut line with a soap bar to lubricate the blades with each snip.

For quicker cutting of angle iron, start at the point of the "V."

To make it easier to cut pipe or conduit on a saw-horse, make a "V" notch in the top rail. You can hold the pipe in place.

You can saw through corrugated metal roofing with a circular saw much better if you install the blade backwards.

Drilling holes 🔒

To start a hole in sheet metal without the bit skidding across the surface, put a tab of masking tape over the spot and drill through the tape.

Make a drill guide from a plastic plate scraper with a V-notch cut in the end. With the bit in the "V" a little pressure will keep it in place.

To drill a cleaner hole in thin sheet metal, sandwich it between wood scraps.

If you need a hole in which a sheet metal screw will go, you may do better to punch it. This leaves more metal for the threads to engage.

The drill bit may heat up when going into metal or masonry. Keep a water pistol filled with light oil handy to squirt on the bit and cool it.

After drilling a blind hole, use a magnetized screwdriver to remove all the filings from the hole. If you try to blow them out, you'll get one in your eye.

Rust removal

Dry Portland cement plus a dry rag will take most rust off metal.

Or, dip a commercially soaped steel wool dish pad in kerosene instead of water and rub the rust away. 👓

Wire

Getting kinky

Often you can straighten out a length of wire by weaving it back and forth between the tines of a garden rake. Then pull the wire and as it goes through, it'll straighten out.

Rope and Cord

Unraveling?

Put a dab of silicone sealant on rope ends to prevent it from becoming frayed.

Plastics

Cutting remarks 👓

If cutting plastics where the protective paper has been removed, run masking tape along the intended cut line on both sides.

Scratches

Some scratches can be removed from clear plastic with jeweler's rouge or other very fine buffing compounds.

An armor coat

Protect plastic surfaces with a coat of auto paste wax.

Chemicals and Shop Compounds

Out of date? ☠

Use a date stamp on chemicals and compounds so you know when purchased. This lets you use oldest first and use up those with limited shelf life.

The hang-up

Compounds in boxes can be made handier by taping a giveaway wooden paint paddle to the box. Drill a hole and hang it from a hook.

Aerosol sprays

Many cleaning concoctions come in convenient aerosol cans, but if the nozzle gets clogged, the convenience is gone. Many of the plastic tips are interchangeable, so borrow one from another can. Keep spare nozzles soaking in solvent and you'll always have a clean one.

The mix-up

Rather than stirring to mix, some shop compounds can be poured into a zip-up plastic bag and either shaken or kneaded to mix. Throw the bag away when the chore is done.

If you're getting flack for using bowls and lids from the kitchen for mixing in the shop, line the containers with plastic so that none of the mix touches the container.

Or, use aluminum foil.

A wire potato masher is a great hand mixer for the shop.

Or, maybe you prefer a wire whisk.

The old-fashioned hand crank egg beater is a world beater!

No mixing bucket? Use a corrugated box with a sheet of plastic as a liner.

When mixing acid and water, always pour the acid into the water so that if there are any splatters, it'll be water that splashes out.

Often you can avoid lumps by adding powder to the water rather than vice versa.

Too fast?

If the compound is setting up faster than you can use it, try adding a couple of pinches of sugar to the next batch to slow it down.

Some folks add a little vinegar.

Another retarder is to add a drop of liquid detergent per pint of water.

Or, use a tablespoon of borax per quart of water.

When mixing plaster of Paris, one-third teaspoon of cream of tartar per gallon will make it set more slowly.

Water putty
Add a tablespoon of milk per cup of water putty powder to slow the setting time.

Make water putty okay for use outside by adding an ounce of linseed oil per half pound of the powder.

Glazier's putty
Reclaim dried putty by putting it in a zip-up plastic bag along with some linseed oil. Put the bag in hot water and work it around with your hands. The heat and oil will bring new life to the blob.

Lubrication

Machine oil formula 🔥
Make your own machine oil by mixing a tablespoon of kerosene with four tablespoons of mineral oil.

Free lubricant
Grease left over from cooking can be a good lubricant for drill bits and other things.

Penetrating oil
A must for the home shop for use on stubborn screws and bolts. If you have a problem but no penetrating oil, here are some great substitutes: vinegar, hydrogen peroxide, kerosene, household ammonia, carbonated beverage, lemon juice, and iodine.

If penetrating oil doesn't work, apply heat from a torch or other heat source and tap a few times.

Applying the lube
If the spout from the oiler can't reach the spot that needs oil, try inserting a straightened-out paper clip wire into the spout. The oil will follow the wire.

When the opening in the spout is too large, close it with fingernail polish and then poke in a pin to reopen with a smaller hole.

A muselege bottle with a slit in the rubber cap that forms a push-on applicator can be cleaned and filled with oil for easy application.

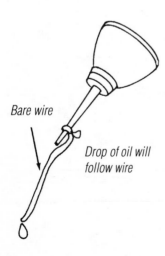

Bare wire

Drop of oil will follow wire

HARDWARE

Nails

Splitting boards?

Drill a pilot hole in the wood and there'll be no splitting as the nail goes in.

Blunt the point of a nail with a tap and it will be less likely to split the board.

Keeping the nails handy

Add a handy nail holder to your shirt cuff, the right sleeve if you're right handed. Just apply a strip of double-faced carpet tape around the cuff. You'll still have the use of both hands, but when you start nailing, you can pluck nails out individually for a quick and easy job. You may become the fastest nailer in town.

Stick an assortment of small nails into a cork kept in the tool box. It may save a few trips back to the shop.

Or, put the assortment in a plastic pill bottle.

Ever hear of the "carpenter's cuff?" Carpenters buy overalls that are too long and fold up the bottom of a leg. This becomes a pocket for nails that is very handy when working in a kneeling position.

Invisible nail heads

You can hide nail heads if you start a chisel into the wood to raise a shaving. However, don't take it all the way off. Drive the nail under the shaving and then glue it back to hide the nail completely.

Lost your head?

If the head comes off from trying to remove the nail, grab it with vise-grip pliers close to the surface and use your claw under the visegrips.

Hitting the wrong nail?

Avoid hitting your thumbnail when hammering in small nails and tacks by letting a paper clip hold the nail while you hold the clip.

Or, use a bobby pin, a slit soda straw, a slit business card, or a slit pencil eraser.

Maybe you like the idea of a magnetized thimble from the sewing room. You may still hit the wrong nail but it'll be wearing armor.

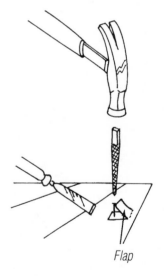

Flap

Bobbie pin holds nail

Slit in eraser

Magnet against plastic.
When removed, all parts
fall into container

Ouch!
If you hit the wrong nail, apply toothache medicine to the finger or thumb as soon as possible for less pain.

Don't cry over spilled nails
Let a magnet pick them up quickly. So you don't have to spend an hour making the magnet let go, put the magnet on a plastic bag. When all the nails are up, turn the bag inside out and they're in the bag.

Or, place the magnet against a plastic butter container lid. The nails will be drawn up against the lid and when it's put in place and the magnet removed, the nails are back at home.

Screws

Chewed up slot
When the slot of a screw has become botched, use a hacksaw to cut a new one at right angles to the old.

Screw storage
An old plastic ice tray makes a nice container for storing screws and other small parts.

A good storage container for screws is a section of plastic pipe with caps on each end. Use a felt marker to label the contents.

Deodorant jars are good for storing tiny screws as the curved bottom makes picking them up easier.

Fast draw
Make a holster for screws by cutting a pair of slits in a paper cup. Fit your belt through the slits.

The easy way
Stick the screw in a candle stub and it'll go in easier and also be somewhat protected against moisture.

A bar of soap does the same thing.

Or, a chapstick is handy for this.

Slits

Keep 'em tight
Put a tiny piece of rope caulk in with each screw before tightening. This keeps moisture out and helps the screw hold tighter.

Keep the tiny screws on eyeglasses tight with a dab of clear nail polish.

Nuts and Bolts

A tightening tour
Fasteners have a way of working loose from vibration or maybe "just because." It's a good idea to take a periodic tightening tour, checking every nut, bolt, and screw in the house.

Storage
Everybody ends up with a can of miscellaneous nuts and bolts. Pour them out onto a dustpan. It'll be easier to find what you're looking for and then easy to pour everything back into the can.

Or, keep the miscellany in a salt carton with a flip-out spout. You can pour the contents out a few at a time and it's easier to find what you need. Use a small funnel to get the stuff back in.

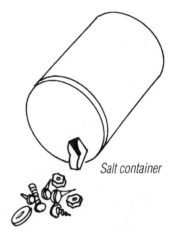
Salt container

Make an ideal tote for an assortment of nuts and bolts by adding a screen door handle to an old muffin pan.

Better wrench hold
If a wrench is a tad loose on a nut, take up the gap with a layer or two of plastic sheet.

When using an open-end or box wrench in a hard-to-reach place, hold the nut in place with a piece of tape across the back of the wrench and the nut.

Rounded corners
When the nut is too worn, install a second nut turned down tight against the first. Now your wrench can grab both and usually they both come off together.

Locking it in place
Tighten the nut over a tab of plastic around the bolt threads and it's as good as having a lock washer.

Shortening a bolt
Cutting off a bolt often leaves a burr. Prevent this by leaving a nut on between the cut and the head. After cutting the bolt, remove the nut and it'll remove the burr.

The stubborn nut

Penetrating oil will run off of a vertical surface before it can do much good. Make a sort of bandage over the nut with a rag and masking tape to hold the liquid in place.

WONDERFUL WORKSHOP IDEAS

Safety

What not to wear

Rings and other jewelry can be dangerous when using some power tools. Put a bright plastic hook on the shop wall as a place to hang your jewelry while working.

What to wear

Use a foam head made for wigs as a place to keep your hard hat, goggles, ear plugs, and mask. Put it in a prominent place so you'll always be reminded.

When you need a hard hat, a child's football helmet can save the day.

A swim mask can protect your eyes when safety goggles aren't around.

Fire safety 6

Spontaneous combustion can happen when oily rags are left exposed to the air. Metal cookie tins with slip-on tops will store them.

Don't leave oily work clothes or gloves out. Either wash 'em or can 'em.

Workbench

Need an anvil?

If you have occasional need for an anvil, the sole plate of a discarded iron can be mounted on one corner of your bench.

Or, for a mini anvil, use a railroad spike dropped into a square hole in the bench top.

If you attach a piece of angle iron along the front edge of the workbench, you have an anvil area plus great protection for the edge, which takes quite a beating. This also provides a lip to prevent things from rolling off.

There's a hitch

An unused trailer hitch can be removed from the car and installed on the workbench to become a handy anvil.

Controlling the bench

To avoid "wandering workbench," install screen door hooks at each end of the bench. Install the eyes at the proper place on the wall and the bench is hooked in place.

Handy alternations

Drill a hole in a side edge of the bench as a convenient place for a pencil.

If your bench has drawers, use door knobs instead of the regular pulls. They're much heftier.

More work space

Cover an old ironing board with a plastic drop cloth to add to the work space in a shop.

Ouch!

Ever pull a drawer out too far and have fifty pounds of tools hit your foot? Paint red lines on the drawer at the point beyond which the drawer could fall out.

Take note

Spray a window shade with chalkboard paint for a pull-down note board in front of the bench.

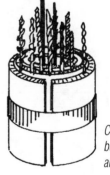

Corrugated board around can

Shop Storage

Small parts

Cut off the top of a plastic bottle and punch a pair of holes near the lip of the bottom. This handy bin for small parts hangs from the shop wall.

Rivet a pop-top pull ring into the lip of a can and there's another hang-up bin.

A large safety pin will hold a good supply of metal washers and hang from the shop wall.

Tool holders

A tight roll of corrugated board in a can will allow you to poke several screwdrivers in between corrugations. Drip candle wax in and the screwdriver is protected from rust.

PVC pipe holds screwdrivers

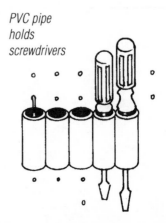

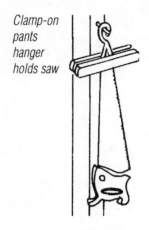

Clamp-on pants hanger holds saw

Glue several short sections of PVC pipe together and then hang this screwdriver rack to the wall with a pair of holes for hooks.

Make slots in the edge of a shelf to hold files.

A clamp-on pants hanger can hold the end of a saw blade and hang it from the wall.

Cut slits in adjacent studs for a saw blade to fit into.

Screen door springs attached horizontally to the wall will hold many flat or small items.

Make a sleeve from a small tin can and attach it to a workbench leg to hold a hammer.

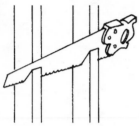

Hooked on hanger-ups

Cut away parts of a wire coat hanger and form it as shown to become a sturdy wall hook.

If you have exposed studs, staple chicken wire across several of them. Make wire hooks from which you can hang all sorts of tools.

Derust tools |6|

Mix a quart of 20w motor oil with two quarts of kerosene, and soak all metal tools for at least two days. They'll be rust-free.

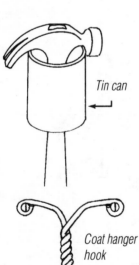

Tin can

Guarding the bottles

If you have a shelf holding glass bottles, make a guard rail around the front of the shelf with curtain rods.

Quieter

Staple or glue scraps of foam-type carpet padding inside drawers to be easier on the tools and quieter on your ears.

Coat hanger hook

String along

Make a string dispenser from a two-liter plastic bottle by cutting off the bottom. Mount it upside down on the shop wall with the string coming out the spout.

Or, punch a hole near the bottom of a coffee can for the string to run through and mount it on the wall.

Or, use a plastic berry basket.

For a ball of twine that unrolls from the center, fit a wide rubber band around the ball and feed the string out through a hole in the band. The string won't hop around and run away from you.

Use a nut pick to help untangle and unknot string or cord.

Hinge storage
Store hinges with their screws sticking outward and use a rubber band to hold everything together.

Lumber storage
Line up old tires hung from the ceiling and they'll hold lots of long lumber and pipes.

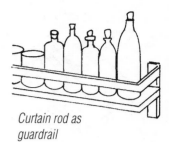

Curtain rod as guardrail

Lighting

Free Light
Paint the floors and walls of the shop a light color or white. Reflected light is free and aids in your visibility.

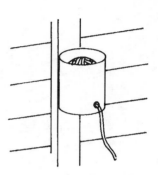

String dispenser

Comfort

Agony of de-feet
Use a strip of leftover carpet along the full length of the bench for greater foot comfort.

Clean Up

Grime doesn't pay
Rub petroleum jelly over your hands before starting a project. Dirt and grime cannot get into the pores and will be easier to clean.

Another invisible glove formula is to blend one part melted wax with three parts petroleum jelly.

Scrape a dry bar of soap with your fingernails and grime can't get under the nails.

Sprinkle talcum powder on your hands before you start and less grime will stick to the hands.

A cheap shampoo for oily hair will also remove oil from your hands.

Work mayonnaise into grimy hands and then wipe away.

Prewash from the laundry room does a good job on grimy hands.

String

Wide rubber bank helps control string

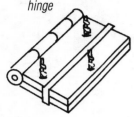

Screws stored with hinge

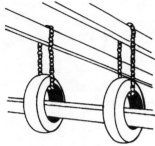

Old tires suspended from rafters become rack for lumber

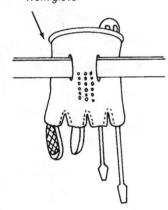

Work glove

Or, mix sawdust into liquid detergent to get rid of handyman hands.

Make your own hand cleaner. Mix one cup cornmeal, one cup powdered detergent, and a half cup baking soda. Wet your hands and work it in.

Use double-sided tape to attach a handy box of tissues to the bottom of a shelf with the tissue sticking down.

If you're lucky enough to have a sink in your shop, put all soap slivers in a nylon stocking which hangs down into the sink.

Work Clothes and Gear

Here's a hand with gloves

Work some silicone sealant around into the palms of your work gloves. When this stuff sets up, you'll have a much better grip on life, as well as many other things.

The right glove wears out quicker than the left in most cases. Save the lefties and turn them inside out to become right gloves for extended wear.

Rubber gloves will come off easier if you dust the insides with a generous amount of talcum powder before you start to work.

A worn-out glove can be converted into a handy holster for small tools. Cut off the tips of the fingers and make two slits for a belt to fit through. Drop the tools into the finger openings.

On the spot

Mix a paste of cream of tartar and water and smear over rust spots on work clothes. When it dries, run through the washing machine. No more rust.

Hang up dirty work clothes wrong side out so dirt won't be transferred to anything they touch.

Longer wear

Coat the edges of pockets with clear fingernail polish for longer wear as these spots start to fray before most others. Also, coat the wear areas of your shop apron.

Or, use a dab of silicone sealant.

For longer wearing work clothes, press an iron-on patch to the underneath side of heavy-wear areas.

Give extra life to pockets where nails and other

sharp objects will be carried by turning the pants wrong side out and applying a denim iron-on patch over the bottom of the pockets.

APARTMENT DWELLERS

No Workshop?

A workbench
Cut plywood to a size that will be a generous bench top. Then install a pair of wooden cleats underneath to fit into the kitchen sink. Position these so they'll fit snugly. The bench top won't be able to move around while in use.

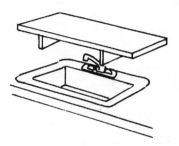

A folding ironing board covered with a plastic drop cloth will serve as an apartment workbench.

Sane sanding
Rather than fill your apartment with sanding dust, put the work inside a plastic bag from the dry cleaners. Stick your hands in and you'll be able to see what you're doing but the dust can't get out.

No Tool Storage?

It's in the box
An extra bread box can house all the tools you'll need for coping with small repairs.

Safety and Security

SAFETY

Child-Proofing

Controlling the crib
Install a pair of screen door hooks and eyes to hold the crib to the wall to prevent the crib from "walking" to some spot where the child might be able to reach something unsafe.

Swing safely
Make the swing set tip-proof by setting each leg in the center of an old tire, fill the space with rubble and then pour concrete in to fill the tire.

> The wear on the chain of a swing set is greatest where the chain is hooked to the eyebolt at the top. Add safety chains to those already on a swing set. The safety chains are just a few lengths long and are attached to an eyebolt a few inches from each already there. If the chain breaks the safety takes over.

Tires and concrete anchor swing set

Sliding glass door safety
Put decals on sliding glass doors down at the child's eye level so there's less danger of trying to run through what is thought to be an open door.

Keeping kids away from tools
To prevent a child from being able to open a drawer in a shop, drill a hole through the top of the bench just inside the drawer's back end. Drop a bolt in the hole. Now the drawer can't open.

The wading pool
To keep kids from slipping and sliding, install bathtub appliques to the bottom of the plastic pool.

Smoke Alarms and Fire Safety

Life savers
Test the batteries in your smoke alarms at least twice a year. A good way to remember is to check them when daylight savings time goes off and on. As soon as you reset the clocks, check the alarms.

Just like school days
Hold a fire drill and let everyone know the various escape routes.

SECURITY

Hardening the Target

Say what?
"Hardening the target," a term used by police, means making it more difficult for a crook to gain entry into your home. Usually a burglar wants to spend only a few minutes trying to get in and if there's a snag, will move on to another house.

    Always keep doors and windows locked.

    Storm windows and storm doors make an extra barrier.

Check for fingerprints
If you have a key-pad combination lock to gain entry to your home, clean the buttons from time to time. Otherwise oil from the fingers will identify the numbers in your combination.

Casement windows
Once the glass in a casement window is broken, thieves can reach in and crank the entire window open. Remove the cranks to slow them down.

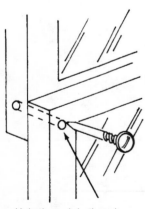

Hole through both sashes

Regular windows
With the window closed, drill a hole through the frames where the upper and lower sash meet. Don't go all the way through to the outside. With a sturdy nail in the hole, the window cannot be raised.

Tamperproof screws

Make screws tamperproof by flowing solder into the screw slot. If you ever need to loosen the screw, you can easily melt the solder.

Patio doors

Sliding glass patio doors are often easy to open, even when locked. Improve your chances with a broom handle or iron pipe in the track where the door slides.

If there's much up and down movement in the door panel, it may be enough for the crook to just lift up and move the panel over the track. Install sheet-metal screws in the upper track. Let them stick down as far as possible without the door touching them.

Or, open the door and slide a metal rod in the top track. Fasten it to the upper track with a hot glue gun.

Drill a hole through the track and into the door so a large nail can go in. This means the door can't move up, down, or sideways with the nail in place. Tie a string around the nail head so it can hang in place until needed.

An adaptation of both the bar and the nail can work in windows.

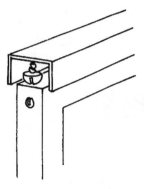

Screws in track make lifting door from frame impossible

Dead solid

All entry doors should have dead bolt locks.

Crude but effective

If the entry door opens to face a wall, measure the distance from the door to the wall and cut a 2x4 to fit. With this bar in place, the door cannot be opened.

See who's there

Solid entry doors should have a viewer so you can see who is there before opening the door.

An attached garage

You'll also want to see who is in the garage, so install a viewer in the connecting door as well.

If your garage door is on a track, a C-clamp attached to the track just above a roller will mean the garage door can't be raised.

2x4 against entry door and opposite wall

Your Valuables

Make a record

Use your video camcorder to make a tape of all your valuables such as jewelry, silver, furs, TV sets, and everything else that you treasure. As you shoot, tell about make, model, serial numbers, and anything else you can think of. Keep it in a safety deposit box in case of fire or theft.

If you don't have the video equipment, take snapshots and either write the description or talk into a cassette recorder.

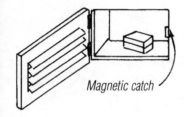

Fake vent is safe

Magnetic catch

A hot spot for hiding

A fake heating vent can be held in place by magnets and allow you to store goodies in the hollow space between walls.

Plug into this one

Dummy electrical wall outlets are also a way to fool the crook.

Who steals old paint?

Pour some leftover paint in a jar and swirl it around to coat all the insides with paint. Pour the paint out and, when dry, the jar will be opaque. Put valuables in and store it on a high shelf.

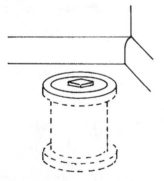

A plumb clever idea

In a basement or utility room, set a section of large plastic drain pipe in the wall with a clean-out plug on one end and a cap on the other. Done right, this "safe" will look right at home.

Capped plastic drain with removable plug is floor safe

Be Prepared

Light up

Attach a magnetized flashlight to the metal bed frame so you can get into quick action if you hear noises. A burglar trying to break in isn't going to stick around if there's someone up and moving around.

A Place for Everything and Everything in Its Place

STORAGE AND SPACE

Where Is What?

A storage journal
If you're a pack rat, like I am, you may forget where you stowed some of your valuable junk. Why not start some kind of a loose-leaf notebook entitled "Where it's at" and jot down everything you stash.

Closets

Don't spare the rod
Add a rod halfway down and put all short items on that side of the closet.

Chain and hanger hint
Hang a length of chain from one wire hanger. Each link can receive another hanger. Takes up much less space.

Add a shelf
Most closets have a shelf on each side. There's usually room to add a shelf at each end.
    If the shelf above the hanger rod has enough space, double deck.

Add a few hooks
Most closet doors will have only one coat hook inside. Why not add several more to handle belts, ties, and lots of other small items.

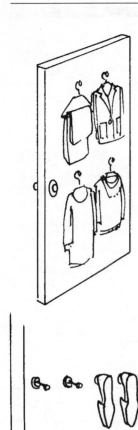

Behind closed doors
Or, pegboard can be installed to the inside to allow for dozens of hanging things.

Belt bits
Install cup hooks in the bottom of a wooden hanger to hold belts.

Hang your shoes
Shoes can be hung from screw-in doorstops installed inside a closet door.

Humidity fighters
Put a few charcoal briquettes in a bowl and they will absorb moisture from the air in a closet.

A container of cat litter will also help . . . unless the cat gets into the closet.

Install louver panels in the door to allow air to move in and out of the closet.

Use a small light to help dry out the air.

Corrugated boxes used for off-season clothes can be made humidity-resistant by spraying with shellac.

Party time
If you need extra hanging space for a party, fold a three-panel screen into a U-shape and place a metal towel bar across the top.

Or, install a pair of screw eyes in a corner connected by a chain from which hangers can hold coats.

Table leaves
Hang table extension leaves on the wall behind the clothes. They take up no room, are hidden, and are better protected from scratches.

The hefty hanger
Strengthen flimsy wire hangers by taping two or more tightly together.

Hang-ups for kids
In a kid's room, install rods low enough so the child learns to hang up things.

The lighter touch
Improve the light conditions in a dark closet by painting walls and all with a glossy white enamel.

A more efficient cedar closet
Use weatherstripping all around a cedar closet to contain the cedar door.

Too much closet space?
Convert a guest closet into a bar with a few shelves, a chest top for mixing, and an ice chest.

Stair Storage

The simple way
The space below your stairs is great for all sorts of storage (unless they are open stairs). Just install a door for access.

Take advantage of every inch of space by making triangular shelf units on rollers.

Step-by-step storage
Make a step near the back door into a storage bin by hinging it so it can be raised. Great for boots, balls, and sporting gear.

Or, install pull-out drawers in the risers.

Drawers under each step

Under the Bed

Out of sight
Make roll-out bins to fit under the beds. They're good for linens, toys, and lots of other things.

Wall Storage

Picture perfect
Like a hidden wall safe, hinge a wall hanging to hide a space cut into the wall between two studs. Just add shelves.

Artful storage
Glue an attractive poster to the top of a bridge table and store it in plain sight as a wall hanging. Varnish the poster for protection.

No Garage?

Carport storage

If you're an apartment dweller, buy second-hand school lockers. Attach these to the carport posts with the fasteners inside. When locked, the stowed things will be fairly secure.

Shelf Paper

Erase the wrinkles

If you're having trouble smoothing that stick-on shelf paper, try smoothing with a blackboard eraser.

Have a fit

For an exact fit of shelves and drawer bottoms, make a paper pattern.

Let go!

Removing stick-on shelf paper is sometimes very difficult. Use a hand-held hair dryer in one corner. The heat softens the adhesive and you can then start to peel it up. If there's still some adhesive left, spritz it with a laundry pre-wash spot remover. After about twenty minutes, the glue will wipe right up.

Instant Shelves

Quick shelves

Well stacked

Everybody knows about the instant book shelf idea where you use a stack of bricks or concrete blocks at each end as spacers between shelves. Give it a touch of class by covering the spacers with fabric or leftover wallpaper.

Or, use rectangular clay flue tiles as spacers.

The Cedar Closet

Moths?

Cedar odor does not kill moths; it only repels them. Clean all clothes before storing in a cedar closet or chest.

An option to the cedar closet
If you don't have a cedar closet, new plastic trash cans are ideal. Put in moth crystals as you pack.

A cedar drawer
Leftover cedar slat scraps can be used to make a cedar-lined drawer or two.

Creating Space

Bag it
Between trips, suitcases will hold many stored items.

Inner space
The area between studs can be converted to a pantry or another cabinet. After all, that's the way most bathroom medicine cabinets get their space. (Don't try this on an outside wall which should have insulation inside the walls.)

A hall wall
Almost every hallway offers a long wall. You can add open shelves up about a foot from the ceiling without taking away from the width of the hall. If the hall is wide enough, you could install floor-to-ceiling shelves.

Under the bed
Make roll-out bins for storage under the bed. This idea also makes a good toy storage plan for a child's room.

In the bed
Store extra blankets between the mattress and the springs.

Linens

Makes scents
Unwrap a bar of scented bath soap to store among seldom-used linens to keep away the musty smell.

HANG IN THERE

Pictures

In the right spot

In hanging a picture, when you decide on the right spot, wet the end of your finger and "hang" the picture wire on your finger. Press the wall and the damp spot will tell you where to place your hanger.

Or, make a paper pattern of the frame, pin it up, and step back to decide if that's where it belongs. If so, mark it by poking a pencil through.

No flaking walls

Place a strip of masking tape over the spot to be nailed to prevent plaster from crumbling.

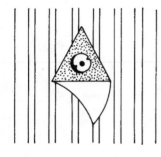

No Nail Holes

"V" for victory

Before hanging a picture on a papered wall, cut a "V" in the paper where the hanger will go. Dampen this area so you can peel back the "V". When ready to move, remove the hanger, glue the tab back down and the nail hole is gone.

The invisible hang

When hanging from ceiling molding, use nylon fishing line. It's strong and practically invisible.

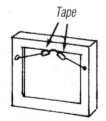

Tape

Hanging straight

A strip of tape wrapped around picture wire on either side of where it hangs from the hook will keep the picture from slipping on the wire and getting cattywampus.

Setting two wall hangers slightly apart will keep a picture straight.

No fingerprints

Putting spacers on the bottom corners of a picture hold it out from the wall. This allows for air circulation which will prevent the picture leaving its imprint on the wall. Thumb tacks make good spacers.

The gang's all here

Wall groupings are popular. Spread a large piece of paper on the floor and arrange the wall hangings on it. When the arrangement is just right, outline each piece and then tape the paper to the wall. You can now make the corresponding nail mark.

When it's time to repaint, take a snapshot of the wall so you can get the grouping back just the way it was. Or, just leave the hooks in place and paint over them.

Frames

Got the wiggles?

Sometimes a loose frame can be fixed by merely driving a staple in each corner making sure the staple spans the joint.

A frame finish

Shoe polish can make an excellent finish for picture frames. It gives color to the wood as well as a protective finish.

Hefty Hangings

Where the studs are

When hanging heavy things like book shelves or even a moose head, it's often best to fasten directly to the studs. How do you find a stud? Tap the wall with a hammer and you should be able to tell the hollow from the solid sounds.

Or, place the side of an electric razor against the wall. Turn it on and as you move it across the surface, you'll detect a different sound where the studs are.

A compass needle will be magnetically pulled over toward nails in the studs as you move it along the wall.

Quick Fixes

DOORS

The "write" way to lube a lock

Get your pencils ready! No, this isn't a magic formula, but it'll make your door locks work like magic. Transfer graphite from a soft lead pencil to the key by rubbing it back and forth. Put the key in the lock and move it in and out several times. Also turn the key back and forth. The lock will love it!

An easy way to sand

If a door drags the floor or threshold, place sandpaper on enough magazines so the door hits the sandpaper. The work the door back and forth over the abrasive.

Dripless lubrication

Use petroleum jelly instead of oil on door hinges. No oil dripping on the carpet.

Stay put

A door that won't stay in the position that it's set in can often be corrected by removing one hinge pin and bending it ever so slightly.

The stubborn hinge pin

To remove a hinge pin, insert a nail into the hole at the bottom of the barrel and drive the pin upward.

The loose hinge screw

One of the main causes of door problems is a loose screw in the hinge. Even one slightly loose screw can let the door sag enough to become hard to close or open. Of course, the first step is to just try tightening.

If the hole is reamed out and the screw can't be

tightened, pack the hole with toothpicks and cut off with a sharp utility knife. The screw goes in just as if it were new wood.

Or, use wooden matches the same way.

Or, coat a wooden golf tee with glue and drive it into the hole. Then cut it off and reinstall the screw.

Sometimes you can wrap a tiny piece of steel wool around the threads and the screw will hold.

Or, wrap the threads with thread and dip the screw into adhesive before reinstalling it.

You can also fill the hole with epoxy glue, coat the screw threads with petroleum jelly, and install the door before the glue starts to harden. However, just push the screw into the epoxy. If you should need to remove the door, the screw will back out.

Removing the door

When taking a door down, remove the bottom hinge pin first and let a wedge hold it level while you work at the top.

Or, let a stack of magazines or newspapers hold it up.

The extra screw trick

You can drill extra holes in the hinge plate for extra screws but you'll have to countersink the extras.

No more slam-bang

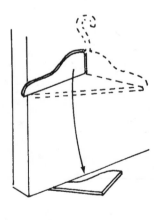

To cut down on slamming noise, put tabs of leftover peel-and-stick foam weatherstripping at several spots all around the doorstop.

Use a wide rubber band around the door knobs on both sides. The part that stretches around the edge will cushion slamming noise. Be sure the rubber band doesn't touch the striker.

For fresh-air fiends, you can stop the wind from blowing a door shut if you install a screen door hook and eye to hold it open.

Or, make yourself some heavy-duty, wooden door-stops by cutting the wedge-shaped ends from a wooden hanger.

Noise can't travel from one room to another if you completely weatherstrip the door just as you would an exterior door.

Door won't latch

If a door doesn't latch, the striker plate opening doesn't line up. To find out where the striker hits, close it with a sheet of carbon paper in between.

Or, cover the striker with chalk or even lipstick, which will leave its mark.

The warped door

A warped door can sometimes be forced back into shape by removing it, placing it on sawhorses, and using weights to straighten it.

On some doors, adding a third hinge in the middle will cure the warp.

Is it sealed top and bottom?

Sometimes the paint or finish isn't put on the top or bottom edge. This means the door can take in moisture from the air and swell. Check and seal all door edges.

A clever way to coat the bottom without removing the door is to use a strip of carpet. Brush the finish on the top side of the carpet and then slip in under the door. Work it back and forth as you work from the front edge to the hinge edge.

All swollen up

When a door doesn't open or close because it has swollen, before you get out the plane, try using a hand-held hair dryer on the places that stick. Remove the moisture and the swelling goes. Seal the area to keep future humidity from getting to the wood.

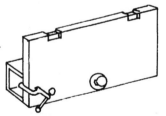

Wooden box holds door steady for planing, plane sides towards ends. Plane hinge side if possible.

Plane and fancy

When you remove a door for planing, clamp a wooden apple crate to each end and the door will stand by itself.

Ride 'em, cowboy!

If a door is removed to plane the top or bottom, just straddle it to keep it steady.

The new door

When hanging a new door, use a single-edge razor blade to outline the hinges. Tap it with a hammer to get the needed depth. Your chisel will stop at these lines.

Damage control

Repair a hole or gouge in a slab door with auto-body filler. When it sets up, you can sand it smooth and then paint over it to completely hide the repair.

It it's an interior painted door, you can fill a gouge with water putty.

The obstacle course

A door that sticks out in the way may become less obtrusive if you just mount it to swing the other way.

Or, replace it with a pair of bi-fold door panels that open at the center.

The baby's room

Install a door viewer on the nursery door to let you look in without waking up the baby.

If you have pets that you want to keep away from the baby, install a screen door with a spring for self-closing. You can hear what's happening but the pets can't get in to lick the child.

A-door-able treatments for old doors

Plastic laminate, like that used on countertops, can be applied to a flush door to make it look new. A paneled door will have to be built up in spots to give a solid base for this treatment.

Wallpaper or stick-on shelf paper might be your selection.

Fabric can be stapled to a door. The staples can then be hidden by welting held on by glue from a hot glue gun.

Frames made of decorative molding can make a plain door look more elegant.

The retired swinger

An old slab door may still be of use as a table or bench top.

Sliding door safety

Put a colorful decal on a sliding glass door at just below eye level. It's easy to think a closed door is open and accidentally try to walk through it.

WINDOWS

Cleaning

Togetherness

Do window washing as a couple. The person outside uses only horizontal strokes and the person inside uses only vertical strokes. It's easy to see which side the streaks are on. If you have to do the job solo, this idea will still work.

Make your own cleaner [6]

Here's a good window cleaner formula. Mix two cups kerosene into a gallon of warm water. It cleans away lots of stubborn spots. When the glass is wiped, the kerosene leaves an invisible film that lets water bead up and run off.

Or, to a gallon of warm water, add 1/2 cup of ammonia, one cup of white vinegar, and two tablespoons of cornstarch.

Try three tablespoons of denatured alcohol per quart of warm water.

Double your pleasure by making a double bucket for window cleaning. Put a two-pound coffee can filled with water in the bucket. Pour the cleaning solution in the bucket around the coffee can, making sure its level is below the top of the can. Only one bucket to carry!

A tea party for windows

Leftover tea is a super window and mirror cleaner. The stronger the better.

Start spreading the news

Better wear your Foster Grants because windows gleam when the final wiping is done with wadded up newspaper. Use a clothespin to attach a grocery bag to your belt to hold the used papers.

Try a blackboard eraser. It also does a good polishing job.

Cleaning windows by long distance

A hose-end sprayer and automatic dishwasher liquid make an easy job of second-story windows.

Be shady

Don't do windows in full sunshine because the sun dries the cleaner before you have time to shine up the glass.

Broken Glass

Paneful repairs

Minor scratches may be removed from glass with jeweler's rouge.

A BB gun hole in a window pane can be filled with clear fingernail polish. Dab, wait to dry, and dab again until the hole is filled.

Clear shellac will also work.

Use the same trick on stained glass. You'll probably find a polish the same color as the glass.

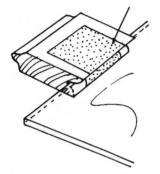

Glass-cutting cuts

After cutting glass panes to fit, remove the sharp edges with sandpaper. For this purpose, a sanding block made from a scrap of tongue and groove flooring is great! The sandpaper fits into the grooved part and sands both sides while keeping your hands away from the sharp edges.

Tongue and groove flooring piece is sanding block for edge of glass.

Wear rubber gloves to handle glass panes. You get a better grip, full dexterity, and no fingerprints or blood stains.

Leather work gloves will also protect your hands.

The pick-up trick

Use a rubber suction cup to help life panes of glass.

The glass cut-up

Store your glass cutting tool in a plastic toothbrush holder.

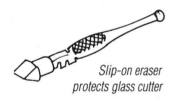

Slip-on eraser protects glass cutter

Or, push one of those slip-on pencil erasers over the cutter wheel.

A spent shotgun shell with a little oil in the bottom makes a good receptacle to house your glass cutter.

To the point

If you run out of glazier's points, the little push-pins that hold the pane in place until you putty over them, use a small dab of glue from the hot glue gun.

The putty problem

Hardened putty can be softened with heat from a propane torch, solder iron, or heat gun. Sometimes you can even use a hair dryer.

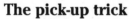

If you have more time, brush the putty with linseed oil.

Before installing new glass, it's a good idea to brush all of the parts where putty will touch the wood with linseed oil. This prevents the wood from drinking the oils from the putty.

When using a putty knife, prevent the putty from sticking by dipping the blade in sudsy water.

Or, have a rag dipped in linseed oil and wipe the blade often, leaving a thin film of oil.

Before capping up a can of glazier's putty, pour about ¼ inch of water into the can to cover the surface. No air gets to the putty so it doesn't dry out.

The last step
After a couple of days, paint over the new putty, sealing it completely. The paint should seal all the way over the edge of the putty and onto the glass.

Lubrication
Rub a candle stub into the tracks for easier window movement.

Or, use a bar of soap.

Shades

Tension headache
Window shades that act up can be fixed by adjusting the tension. A shade that can't make it back up needs more tension. Pull the shade down, take it out of the brackets, and hand roll it back up about two revolutions. If it still hasn't got what it takes, do it again.

For the shade that goes flying back up, relieve the tension by unrolling it by hand a couple of turns; that should tame it.

Patch work
Often a small tear can be mended with masking tape on the back and clear nail polish on the front.

The artful way to clean
An art gum eraser will clean many spots from a shade.

Your Screen Test

A grand opening

A small hole in a screen can be closed with clear nail polish. First, use an ice pick to pull the wires back in place as best you can.

Shellac will also patch a hole.

Model airplane glue will also work.

Many plastic screens can be patched by using a piece of screening to cover the problem and running a medium hot iron over the patch. It will melt and fuse together to cover the hole.

Screen paint

When painting the frames on screens, mask the screen or the paint will fill up the tiny openings.

Use a blackboard eraser to paint screens.

Here's a technique that works. Brush on the paint on one side and, before it has time to dry, use a dry brush on the other side. Enough paint will have come through, and this way you have no clogged openings.

Blind Spots

Put on the gloves

Wear cotton gloves to wash blinds. Your fingers do a better job than a brush.

Now where was I?

If you have to stop in the middle of the job, clip a clothespin on the last slat you've cleaned so you'll know where to start again.

Cleaning

The tub is a good place to clean blinds because the shower can rise them off.

If you hang blinds from the clothesline, you can use the garden hose to good advantage.

To keep the tapes from shrinking, rehang the blinds before the tapes dry.

Hide the gray

White liquid shoe polish will make discolored tapes look new again.

Lubricate the cords
Blinds will work better if you run a candle stub all along the cords making sure to coat all around the cord.

WALLS

A Hole in the Wall

Look, Ma, no cavities
Toothpaste can fill small nail holes in a plaster or textured wall. Sorry, but the kind with fluoride won't prevent future cavities.

Mix thin, almost runny spackling compound and squirt it into tiny holes or small cracks with an eye dropper or plastic squeeze bottle.

Major league damage
For patching larger holes, you need backing. How about a section of window screening cut a little bigger than the hole? Run a wire or string through the center and push the flexible screen through the hole while holding onto the wire or string. Wrap the wire around a pencil and twist the pencil until the screen and pencil are pulled tight against opposite sides of the wall.

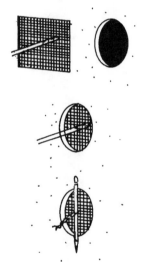

Or, push wadded up newspapers into the hole. When released, they expand and provide backup. Dip the wad in plaster of Paris and the backup will be more sturdy.

Or, cut a piece of corrugated board slightly larger than the hole. Poke a hole through the center of this and insert a balloon. With the open end of the balloon facing out, inflate until the balloon holds the corrugated piece tight against the inside wall surface.

Cut a piece of rigid foam insulation to fit into the hole. Taper it down so it can be wedged into the opening. Push it in until flush with the surface and then texture over it.

The no-touch-up way
Mix paint with your spackling compound for patching a hole without having to touch up.

Or, roll up a business card and stick it in the hole. Push it just below the surface. Now take an artist's brush and dab at the hole with matching paint. The hole is filled and it's the right color.

On a white wall, fill a nail hole with correction fluid. This stuff also comes in colors which may match your walls.

Hairline cracks
Use a tiny artist's brush to apply the spackle into these tiny cracks.

No-mess mix-ups
When mixing a small amount of spackling, use half a hollow rubber ball.

Or, use the lid from a sauce pan. The handle makes it easy to hold.

Too fast?
For slow workers, use about one quarter less water, replacing it with white vinegar.

Or, add some sugar or some dry starch to the mix.

Too slow?
If you want to speed it up, add salt.

Do a halfway job
With any of these backings, patch only about halfway to the surface. Let this dry and then finish the job. If you do it all at once, your patch shrinks.

An easy patch
If a solid patch isn't needed, apply strips of self-sticking wallboard tape crisscrossed over the opening. Then texture over this to match the rest of the wall. It's a quick way to do it.

Patching compound formulas
Equal parts of salt and laundry starch with enough water added to make it into a plaster consistency makes a good homemade wall patch.

Or, add talcum powder to white liquid shoe polish until it's thick enough to patch.

Another way to make your own patching compound: Soak several cleansing tissues in white glue. Work them together until they reach putty consistency and patch away.

Or, put strips of newspaper in boiling water until it becomes pulpy. Then squeeze out the water and patch with the pulp. Staples hold tight.

When patching plaster with exposed lath, drive tacks into the wood with the heads sticking up. The patching plaster has something to hold onto.

Smooth joints without sanding

After taping and bedding but before the drywall compound dries, use a towel wet with warm water to smooth. If you do this right, you'll avoid having to sand.

Lots of choices in texturing

Texturing can be done by using a roller to leave a stippled effect. Different lengths of roller nap will leave different patterns.

Swirls can be made with a broom while the drywall compound is still wet.

Use a notched trowel to leave a bold random effect.

Try pressing wet burlap, wadded newspaper, or a damp sponge into the compound.

Any design from geometric shapes to leaves to brick or stone will make a unique texture.

A wire mesh called hardware cloth can be pressed into wet mud and will look like a tiny tile pattern.

Texturing can also be made by mixing sand into the paint.

Test before you paint

The drywall compound must be dry before painting it. To test, tape a six-inch square of plastic to the wall. The next day, if there is moisture under the plastic, you have an excuse to procrastinate for another day. Keep waiting until the wall passes the test.

Cover for the yukky wall

Those 4x5 lattice sections can make a cinder block wall look great. Paint the wall one color and the lattice another. Socko!

Protect the walls

Prevent a chair or sofa from rubbing against the wall by installing a pair of doorstops in the back of the piece so the stops hit the wall instead.

FLOORS

Hiding big damage

For a gouge in vinyl flooring, you can often make a matching patching compound. Use a food grater on a scrap of the vinyl. The resulting chips can be mixed with clear adhesive or shellac to form a paste which can be worked into the gouge.

Or, try a crayon of matching color melted to flow into the hole.

It "seams" like old times

Loose seams on a vinyl floor can often be fixed by running a moderately warm iron over a paper towel placed over the seam. The heat makes the flooring flexible and also activates the adhesive. Put a few books on the seam to weigh it down until the adhesive sets up.

For loose seams around a tile, put a heating pad over the tile and stack books on for weight.

Removing a tile

A damaged vinyl floor tile can often be removed with heat from a torch, iron, or heat gun. Make a slice in the center and apply heat to the center only. Then use a scraper to work under the tile toward the edges, taking care not to damage adjacent tiles.

Or, turn the electric skillet upside down for heating.

Instead of heat, you can also use cold. Place dry ice over the tile to be removed. When it gets cold enough, a good blow with a hammer will cause the tile to shatter. (If dry ice isn't available, fill a bucket with ice cubes and add a few inches of water and some rock salt.)

Rasslin' with a new floor

To tame a large piece of new flooring that doesn't want to uncurl, try laying an electric blanket on it. A little heat may do the job.

Silence!

A squeaky floor is usually caused by two or more boards rubbing together. Stop the movement and you stop the squeak.

This noise can often be silenced by sprinkling talcum powder and sweeping it into the racks.

Liquid wax can be poured and go between the cracks to act as a lubricant.

Or, rub a bar of soap back and forth over the cracks.

If you can get under the floor in a basement or crawl space, wedges between the sub-floor and the joists may be the answer. Good hardwood wedges can be made from wooden clothespins.

Or, use sections of a broken zig-zag ruler. Grind the pieces to a point.

Straighten up
For a warped floorboard, strip the finish and place a damp cloth over it for forty-eight hours. Then use countersunk wood screws to secure the unwarped board.

In the buff
Hang your floor buffer and the brushes won't flatten out.

A wildly different floor covering
When a floor is shot, try this. Cover the surface with a colorful fabric. Even a bedsheet will do. Pull it tight and staple around the edges. Apply a couple of coats of polyurethane and then cover the staples with welting. This can also work for stairways.

STAIRS

For the noisy climber
For a squeaking stairway, install L-shaped metal brackets to the underside to stop movement.

CEILINGS

A mini scaffold
For ceiling work, most of us need just a little extra height. Make a dandy scaffold from a pair of inverted plastic milk cases with a 2x12 across for your walkway.

Here's dust in your eye
When drilling in the ceiling, poke a hole through the center of a throwaway aluminum pie pan. Poke the bit through and let the pan catch most of the dust.

Or, use a plastic butter tub.

Popcorn ceilings

Blown-on acoustical ceilings will often crumble with any cleaning effort. Cover water spots with talcum powder dusted on with a powder puff.

Or, try spraying bleach on the spots. Use a drop cloth to protect your rugs.

Rather than drill in this stuff for hanging baskets, install screw hooks on opposite walls with a wire in between. Paint wire and hooks white and they're almost invisible.

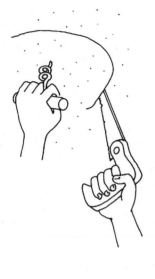

Cutting into the ceiling

If you have to cut into the ceiling, do it from the attic if possible. This allows you to provide a big box underneath to catch dust and you also won't run the risk of cutting through unseen wires.

If cutting from below, insert a corkscrew into the center of the part to be removed. You now have a handle on the cutout.

Patching it

In patching a ceiling hole that requires backing, use a string and weight through the center of the backing piece so gravity holds it in place while you apply the patching compound.

Look up to a great cover-up

Sections of lattice work made for exterior use can be used as a suspended ceiling and will disguise a crummy old ceiling.

Pesky Problems

OUT, OUT, DAMN SPOT

Carpet Stains

A cleaning kit

Every home should have an emergency spot and stain kit for quick carpet help. Include vinegar, carpet shampoo, and cleaners as well as rags and paper towels.

Two magic words

Dab and blot. When you use a cleaner, don't overwet the carpet; just dab it on. As soon as you dab, use a paper towel and blot. Dab and blot, dab and blot.

A stroke of genius

Aerosol shave cream removes many carpet spots.

Always test first

With these or any other solutions to carpet or upholstery spots, always test the cleaner on an obscure spot to see if the solution affects the materials.

Pet stains

Get on these fast. Pick up solids. Blot with a paper towel. Use equal parts white vinegar and water. Dab it on and blot it off.

Or, use club soda.

Or, mix up a solution of baking soda and water.

After cleaning, cover the spot with equal parts of baking soda and salt. After a couple of hours, vacuum it up. If it's still damp, repeat.

Moth crystals sprinkled over the spot can help get rid of the odor. Vacuum it up after an hour or so.

Grease spots

Spread cornmeal over grease spots on a carpet. When vacuumed up the next day, both cornmeal and grease will be gone.

Talcum powder can also work.

Or, sprinkle baking soda.

Acids

Immediately dilute and neutralize any kind of acid spill. Club soda does both. Blot as you apply.

Baking soda and water also dilute and neutralize.

Candle wax

Place a couple of ice cubes in a plastic bag and hold this against the wax. The cold will make the wax brittle and it can be chipped away.

Or, place a blotter or paper towel over the spot and press with a warm iron. The blotter absorbs as the iron melts the wax. Move the blotter as it absorbs.

Chewing gum

The ice-cube-in-the-bag trick also works on chewing gum.

Or, use the old-type cigarette lighter fluid to soften gum.

Ink spots [6]

The alcohol in hair spray will remove some ball point ink marks. Spray and blot. As long as you get any color with the blot, keep going.

Muck and mire

Let mud dry. It can then be loosened with a brush and vacuumed up.

Color gone?

If cleaning takes some of the color from a carpet, replace this with artist's pastels. After a match is made, make a light pass with hair spray to hold the color in.

Or, use permanent felt markers to enhance color. They come in a rainbow of colors.

Scatter borax powder over the rug and wait an hour or so before vacuuming. It may brighten the colors.

Baking soda can be used the same way.

Smoking is hazardous to your carpet

A burned place in a carpet can often be removed by simply snipping off the burned fibers with fingernail scissors. The tiny low spot will probably never be noticed.

If the burn goes down to the backing and the low place does show, pour in some glue and when it starts to get tacky, stand fibers snipped from a scrap into the glue. When the glue sets up, the fibers will look like the original carpet.

Furniture tracks

The mashed-down places will usually come back up by holding a steam iron close to the surface without actually touching. Then work a coin back and forth to raise the pile.

Flooring Spots

Shoe tracks

Heel marks on vinyl flooring can be removed with white appliance wax and a soft rag.

Or, try toothpaste rubbed with a damp rag.

The ordinary pencil eraser can rub out this problem.

Wax applicator tips

A paint pad applies floor wax without getting the goo on baseboards.

Or, use a short-napped paint roller with an extension handle. No bending over.

Start with a well wrung damp applicator and it's less likely to absorb the wax.

Stripping the waxy build-up

Paint thinner removes wax from floors.

Or make this easy wax stripper:

5 cups warm water
1 cup laundry detergent powder
$3/4$ cup ammonia

After the wax is removed, be sure to rinse and dry before rewaxing.

Furniture Spots

The dreaded white ring
Water spots on wood furniture respond to a mild abrasive if it is not used dry. Toothpaste spread over the spot and rubbed with a damp cloth will usually do the job.

Cigar ashes and cooking oil will also rub out water spots.

Or, smear the spot with petroleum jelly and leave overnight.

Mayonnaise works the same way.

Too hot!
Whitish heat marks from a hot dish can be treated just like water marks.

Up to upholstery?
Here's a formula for upholstery cleaner. (As with all cleaners, try it out first on an obscure part of the piece.) Mix one part mild detergent into four parts water. Use a beater to whip up a good head of foam. Use only the foam to brush on the spots. When clean, wipe dry and blot.

Or, use a wet/dry vacuum to remove the moisture.

O D O R S   A N D   M I L D E W

House-a-tosis
Remove odors from the entire house by putting a solid room deodorizer just inside the register of the return air vent for the central heat and air. The fan will pick up the scent and send it throughout the house.

Smoking pollution
Lighted candles help do away with odors — even cigarette smoke smells.

A dish with vinegar will freshen the air in a room full of smokers.

Or, try a saucer with ammonia overnight.

Try this. Take a damp towel and swing it around over your head. It not only does away with snake, it's pretty good exercise.

Wash smelly ash trays with a baking soda and water solution. Use about a tablespoon of soda to a quart of water.

Kitchen odors

For a smelly kitchen, sprinkle cinnamon on a cookie sheet and heat with the oven door open. This will also go throughout the entire house.

Or, use a tablespoon of fresh coffee grounds.

Try boiling water with a little ammonia in it. Just a little!

Cutting boards

Rub salt into the cutting board or butcher block to eliminate food odors.

The sink with bad breath

The sink disposer can develop bad breath. Here are the steps in cleaning it. 1) Pack the unit with ice cubes. When turned on, the cubes will work against the surfaces inside and clean. 2) Put the stopper in and fill the sink with water. Pull the stopper out as you turn on the disposer. This forces more water through than the faucet could. 3) Clean the underside of the rubber splash guard at the mouth of the drain. 4) Feed the disposer half of a fresh lemon.

Instead of regular ice cubes, freeze vinegar or soda plus water and let the disposer chew these for a cleaner, better smelling unit.

Any time you have lemon, lime, orange, or grapefruit peels, let the disposer chew them up.

Let your disposer eat a chopped raw potato to clean the insides.

Out of season

When closing up a fishing cabin or beach house, put a cup of cat litter in all drawers and closets. You won't come back next spring to a musty smell. (However, be sure the cat can't get in or you'll have an even worse odor.)

Don't fall into a trap

When closing up a house or even going on vacation, don't leave traps for mice or rats set. If you catch something, it could create quite an odor before you return.

Mildew

Is it doing you in?
Mildew can be removed from most surfaces by spraying with full strength liquid laundry bleach.

If the surface is of something that would be harmed by bleach, or if you're allergic to bleach, use vinegar instead.

A must for musty odors
Cure a trunk with a musty smell by putting a pound of cat litter inside for two days.

Moldy clothes
On clothing where bleach could remove the color, either dry clean or launder, depending on the fabric.

Try placing the item in the sunshine.

Shoes and bags
On leather goods, clean with equal parts of denatured alcohol and water.

The book of the mold club
If you have a mildewed book, try sprinkling the effected pages with cornstarch.

Outside the house
Here's a formula for getting rid of mildew on exterior surfaces:

> 3 quarts warm water
> 1 quart liquid laundry bleach
> $1/3$ cup of powdered detergent
> $2/3$ cup trisodium phosphate (TSP)

Mix and then scrub the effected surfaces until the mildew is gone. Then rise well.

A closet case
Help prevent mildew in a closet by leaving a 25-watt bulb burning. It helps dry the air.

Or, drill holes in a decorative pattern through the closet door for better ventilation.

Insects

Do roaches bug you?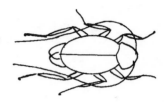
Roaches are the bugs for all seasons. One of the best
home remedies is boric acid powder. Sprinkle it wherever
roaches roam and where the white powder won't show.
The powder doesn't lose its power unless it gets wet.
(Observe all caution notices and keep it away from children and pets.)

Some people prefer this formula:

$1/2$ cup of borax
$1/4$ cup of flour

A variation on this is to add $1/4$ cup of cocoa powder
to the above.

Ants
Without the cocoa, this formula is also said to help con-
trol ants.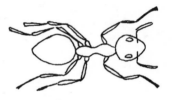

Some claim that bay leaves repel ants after you've
sprayed with insecticide.

If you see carpenter ants, you probably have two
problems: the ants and a leak of some sort. They like wet
wood.

Some old-time ant repellents include grated cucum-
ber peeling, cloves, or fresh coffee grounds.

Flies
A few moth balls in the bottom of your garbage cans will
keep flies from flocking to them.

Or, glue a pest strip to the lid.

Moths
Remember, cedar odor from a cedar closet doesn't kill the
moth, it just helps to repel. If there is no longer the aroma
of cedar, lightly sand the inside walls. This will open the
pores and let the scent come out.

Moths will often attack the pads in a piano. Spoil
their meal by putting moth flakes in the piano. You'll be
able to play it again, Sam!

Keep moth balls in the toe of a nylon stocking to
hang with the clothes.

Weevils
A bay leaf in each container in the spice rack is said to

keep weevils out. It's said to repel other insects as well.

Wasps

If a single wasp or bee gets in the house, a spritz of hair spray will kill it.

Keep wasps from nesting in hollow clothesline poles by plugging the holes with wads of aluminum foil.

Stinging remarks

Tape a can of wasp spray on a long pole. Position a strap hinge above the spray button and tape one hinge plate in place. Run a string through a hole in the other plate. A tug of the string sends a blast of spray into the nest. You still might want to flee the scene.

Mosquitos

Mosquitos breed in stagnant water. Check outside for water in gutters or containers.

Make the bugs go "poof!"

Powder that should go into cracks can be blown in with a plastic squeeze bottle.

Or, put the powder into an envelope and seal it. Then snip a tiny bit off the corner and it will "poof" the powder. Be sure you wet the flap with a damp sponge rather than licking it and maybe some powder.

Rats and Mice

Close the doors

Mice need only tiny cracks to get into your house. Poke steel wool into such openings before caulking.

Or, mix cut up strands of steel wool with spackling compound.

Setting the trap

Traps should be washed and left for twenty-four hours to dry. This does away with the human scent. Then when you get ready to bait them, wear rubber gloves.

If the varmints aren't attracted to the bait on your traps, switch to peanut butter.

Better still, smear peanut butter over a bacon strip.

Try a piece of absorbent cotton. Mice like it for nests.

Soak it in bacon drippings and they'll notice the cotton quicker.

Or, glue dog food to the trap. Rodents love it!

Pet proofing the pest poison ☠

Cut a small hole in the plastic lid from a coffee can. With the poison in the can only the insect or rodent you want can get in.

Minty mouse

It's said that peppermint leaves repel mice. Even if it's not the total eradication of the critters, the leaves do make the house smell nice.

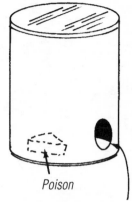

Poison

Opening too small for pets

GENERAL HOUSECLEANING

Broken Glass

A finger saver

Pick up broken glass on hard floors by dabbing with a wet facial tissue.

Toting Supplies

A step saver

A work apron lets you carry all the tools and materials with you to save trips back and forth.

Plastic buckets are lightweight totes for cleaning supplies.

The mobile dispenser

The handle of a plumber's friend will hold a roll of paper towels and will stand by wherever you're working, ready to roll out a towel.

The two-bucket brigade

The second bucket is for cleaning the sponge or rag so the first bucket always yields clean cleaning solution.

Or, if the idea of moving two buckets doesn't grab you, put a large can in the bucket and you still have the same advantage as above but only one bucket to carry.

A sponge pocket

Make a waterproof pocket to hold your sponge by cutting off the top of an old hot water bottle. A couple of slits will let it hang from your belt.

Don't Leave a Clue

No fingerprints

Wear clean cotton work gloves for dusting and never leave a fingerprint.

Or, use a potholder mitt.

Removing fingerprints

Dust oily hand and fingerprints around light switches and door knobs with talcum powder. It absorbs the oil.

Tough Dirt

Easy vase cleaning

Clean down in a hard-to-get-to vase with a denture tablet and water.

The bottle battle

To clean down in a narrow-necked bottle or vase, put in some uncooked rice along with water and detergent. When you shake the bottle, the rice scrubs the insides.

Or, use tacks, toothpaste, and water the same way.

A natural cleaner for artificial flowers

Put a half cup of table salt into a paper bag big enough to hold the flowers. Shake vigorously.

Candle holders

Pop them in the freezer until the wax gets brittle enough to break off.

Chrome cleaner

Try a lemon slice on kitchen and bathroom chrome. Rub, rise, and dry. The shine will amaze you.

Pick up on this one!

If basins and sinks have a metal trim around the top, use a toothpick to clean between the two.

Brooms

Getting dirt out of corners
A whisk broom gets the edges of carpets by moving dirt out where the vacuum can suck it up.

Clean sweep
Soak a new broom in salt water to help it last longer.

Hitting the Dusting Trail

Your sidekick, the feather duster
An old-fashioned feather duster is great because it quickly moves dust from items to the floor where the vacuum can do its thing.

A feather duster inside a metal vacuum cleaner tube can reach up high for dust. It's the best for cobwebs in the corners.

That old paint brush is almost as good as the feather duster.

Slats and louvers
Put a ruler inside a sweat sock and use a rubber band to hold it in place. It reaches between the louvers and gets both sides with one pass.

Energy Users and Energy Savers

PARTS

Help get the right thingamajig
If you can't take the actual part in, write down the part number and name and then take a photograph of the part.

Easy repairs
When making repairs, read the instructions aloud into your tape recorder. Then, as you work, play it back and stop it as need be for the perfect repair.

When taking any appliance apart, you should keep track of the sequence of the parts you're removing. Dictate the sequence into a tape recorder and then play back the cassette to guide you in replacement.

Or, place 'n parts in the proper sequence on a wide strip of tape.

Parts washing
A percolator-type coffee pot works great for parts washing. Put the parts in the coffee holder and lower it into the pot filled with solvent. Work the holder up and down and when you bring it up, the solvent drains out and the parts are clean.

Or, make yourself a percolator parts washer from a big plastic jug with the top cut out and a smaller one with the top cut out leaving the handle. Use an ice pick to poke holes in the smaller jug. Put the parts in the small container and work it up and down in the solvent in the big one.

A paint tray is a good parts washer. Soak 'em in the deep end and use the shallow end as your work area.

Greasing parts
Put bearings and other parts to be greased into a zip-up

plastic bag along with some grease. Now you can work the grease in without getting your hands greasy.

HEATING AND COOLING SYSTEMS

Off-season care
Cover a window unit with a plastic trash bag to keep out the winter cold. Tape it in place with duct tape.

An old shower curtain does the same job.

Keeping the bugs out
Sprinkle moth flakes in the outside condenser/compressor unit to keep wasps from building a nest there.

What's the hold-up?
When installing a window unit, use an auto bumper jack to hold it in place.

Raising humidity
In the winter, humidity is important to your comfort as well as to the belongings in the house. To create humidity, place open containers of water around your home. The water evaporates into the air.

Reroute your clothes-dryer duct into the house to capture the warm humid air.

Thermostats

True or false?
Give your thermostat a lie detector test. Tape a thermometer you know is accurate to the wall next to the thermostat. After a few minutes, compare. If these are more than a degree or so different, either recalibrate or replace your thermostat.

Make certain there is not outside influence on your thermostat—strong lights, a nearby TV, or air movement from fans—that might give false readings.

Radiators

Radiating more heat
Line the wall behind each radiator with aluminum foil, shiny side out. Heat will be reflected out into the room for greater efficiency.

A cleaning hint
Drape a wet sheet or towel over the radiator and use the vacuum cleaner with the hose in the exhaust opening. The exhaust will blow the dirt off and most will stick to the damp cloth. The rest will fall on the floor and then can be vacuumed up.

Water Heaters

No drips
After draining the tank, use a small item called a hose cap to fit over the drain tap on the heater tank to prevent any drips.

No copper here
With a gas heater, many experts suggest not using copper lines to carry natural gas. Even though the gas company tries to clean all impurities from the gas, if some stay in, they can attack the copper and might even eat through it.

Mirror, mirror, on the floor
To aid in lighting or examining the pilot light, put a hand mirror on the floor under the heater.

APPLIANCES

Refrigerators

On the level
The refrigerator or freezer runs more efficiently if the unit is level. Check it front to back and side to side.

Easier moving
To move a big appliance without casters, slide it onto a carpet scrap, pile side down, and it'll slide with ease.

Or, wax the bottom of a large piece of corrugated board. Once you get the unit on this, it's easier to move and easier on the floor.

Air leaks
A faulty gasket can let lots of moisture in and cold out. Check the gasket by closing the door on a $100 bill. (If you're cheap, a one dollar bill will do.) Tug at the bill and if it comes out easily, look at the spot for a problem.

Or, dust blue carpenter's chalk all along the gasket. The chalk will show up inside at any point where the gasket fails.

The best way is to put a strong flashlight into the unit and with the room lights off at night, examine the door. Where you see light, there's a leak.

If the gasket isn't damaged, sometimes you can hold a steam iron close to the bad place. The heat and steam will help a compressed gasket.

Or, rub a thin film of cooking oil on the gasket to improve the seal.

A new gasket
If you are replacing a gasket, replace screws in this manner: Start with the center top screw. Then replace the center bottom screw. Next replace the center side screw on one side and then its opposite on the other side. Keep doing opposites until all are tight. This helps to avoid warping the door.

How cold is it?
In the freezer, use a meat thermometer stuck into a carton of ice cream. It should register zero to 6 degrees (F). Put it in a glass of water in the refrigerator part where it should be 35 to 40 degrees.

P.U.!
Refrigerator or freezer odors can often be absorbed by an open box of soda in each compartment.

Cleaning with a baking soda and water solution will clean and deodorize.

Add a few drops of vanilla extract to water and wipe the walls.

That strange kitchen odor may be coming from the

condensate pan underneath the refrigerator.

Fresh coffee grounds in a cup of cat litter will do away with the odor.

Or, fill the entire compartment with wadded up newspapers and after a couple of days, all odors will be gone.

Clothes Washer

Check for level
This is another appliance that needs to be level to operate best.

Soap Scum
The residue in the machine can be removed by pouring a gallon of vinegar into the empty machine and running it through an entire cycle using hot water.

Eating your clothes?
If clothes are getting snagged, use a nylon stocking over your hand to feel around for the rough place in the tub.

It could be that a zipper is the culprit. Zip up before tossing garments into the wash.

Chips in the tub finish
Chips in the tub finish will lead to rusting. Cover the place with nail polish to keep water out. Silicone sealant will last longer.

Agitated by your agitator?
If the cap holding the agitator on won't budge, maybe an auto oil filter wrench will help.

Dryers

In duct soup
Be sure the exhaust duct doesn't sag or it will trap lint and eventually clog the duct.

Dishwashers

A clean machine
If the dishwasher has a buildup of mineral deposits inside, or if it leaves a film on your dishes, pour a gallon of white vinegar into the machine and run through a wash cycle.

For the off-season
If you're closing up a second home for the season, pour a little water into the dishwasher and then add enough cooking oil to cover the top. The oil prevents evaporation and the water keeps the pump parts from hardening.

Home on the Range

Save a little energy
A self-cleaning oven uses heat for cleaning. Start the cycle after baking when the oven is already hot and save energy bucks.

Spills
Immediately cover spills with salt and when the oven cools, the stuff wipes away with a damp sponge instead of being baked on.

Catch the grease pops
Install a sheet of plastic behind the range to prevent grease from splattering on the wall.

Or, install a washable window shade upside down with the roll hidden by the stove. When needed, pull up the shade and hook it on a cup hook.

Cleaning ceramic cooktops
Pour white vinegar over the brown burner areas of a ceramic cooktop. You will be able to wipe the surface clean in about ten minutes.

Ouch!
Keep an aloe vera plant growing near the stove. You'll find it soothing to rub the gel from the fronds onto minor skin burns.

Oven fire
In case of an oven fire, close the door and turn off the heat and the fire will exhaust itself.

Sink Disposers

Jack of all trades
When installing a disposer, a bumper jack can hold the unit in place while you're getting the connection made.

Trash Compactors

Help from a little extra trash
Put several layers of newspapers flat in the bottom when a new bag is put in. Broken glass will be less likely to puncture the bag. The papers will also absorb any liquids that might become odors.

Also, put a layer of newspapers in on top of bottles that are going to be mashed to contain broken glass.

Steam Iron

What a drag!
An iron that drags during the pressing process can often be cleaned by pressing across a piece of waxed paper on which you've sprinkled salt. Don't do this if your iron is Teflon-coated, but try pressing a piece of aluminum foil.

Silver polish and a damp cloth will also clean the bottom plate.

So will toothpaste.

Run out of steam?
Don't get steamed over a steam iron that spits or doesn't steam. It's usually clogged with mineral deposits. Fill it with white vinegar instead of water. By the time you've steamed out the vinegar, the iron should be back to normal. Since the iron only steams when the plate is facing down, you're probably wondering who is going to hold it for an hour while it steams? Place it on the slotted cover of the oven broiler pan and let it steam into the pan.

If the steam holes are clogged, a pipe cleaner is a good reaming tool.

Vacuum Cleaners

The thread of a good idea
A clogged roller brush makes the unit less efficient. A seam ripper from the sewing room will remove hair and threads very quickly.

Tick-Tock Tips

The noisy electric clock
The whirring will often go away by merely turning the clock upside down and letting it run for a while.

Another equally weird trick for this malady is to put the clock in a barely warm oven for a while. Just be sure it's not warm enough to melt your clock.

Fans

Keep it clean
After oiling a rotating fan, slip a paper bag over the entire fan. Then when you turn it on for the first time, the oil slings out into the bag instead of all over the room.

Batteries Not Included

In cold storage
There are so many battery-powered gadgets that when you see a special on batteries, you should stock up. Store extras in the refrigerator for longer life. Be sure the terminals don't touch anything metal which could discharge them for a premature death.

Doorbells

Louder, please!
If the bell isn't loud enough, place the unit atop a heat duct and the sound will be carried throughout the house.

Chime in
Don't oil a chime unit. Clean the moving parts with rubbing alcohol.

FIREPLACES

Fire Starters

The burning brick trick
Wrap a brick in aluminum foil but before sealing it pour in as much kerosene as the brick will absorb. After a few hours, the brick can be used under your logs as a fire starter.

Better Burning

Keep the home fires burning
Put a layer of foil under the grate so all the ashes will collect there for an easier cleanup.

    Cut some hardware cloth to fit over the grate. As your fire burns, the smaller opening will hold the coals longer before they drop into the ashes. You'll enjoy a longer lasting, warmer fire.

    When burning scrap lumber, nail pieces together for a longer burning "log."

More heat
A few shiny aluminum cans in back of the fire will reflect more heat out.

Soot and Smoke

Root out the soot
If you forgot to open the damper, there are soot marks on the brick outside the fireplace opening. Mix $1/4$ cup of trisodium phosphate (TSP) in a quart of hot water. Wear you rubber gloves and scrub away the smoke damage.

    Washing soda, not to be confused with baking soda, is a strong cleaner. Mix three tablespoons in a quart of hot water and scrub away smoke stains.

    For stubborn spots, make a paste of cream of tartar and water.

To remove smoke damage from a wooden mantel, cover with spray starch. When dry, wipe away with a damp cloth.

Foamy soot removal
Foaming-style bathroom cleanser will also remove smoke stains from brick.

Or, add enough ammonia to a quart of hot water to make it sudsy and use this to scrub away the smoke stains.

Covering your tracks
For soot on a carpet, cover with table salt and after an hour vacuum away salt and soot.

The smell of smoke
Sprinkle nutmeg in inconspicuous areas to mask a smoke odor.

Your fireplace can actually give a pleasant odor to the entire house if you'll just toss dried citrus peels on the fire.

The glass doors
Smoke stains on the glass can be removed by dipping a damp cloth into the ashes and rubbing.

Ashes

The scoop on scooping
One of the best tools for removing ashes from the fireplace is a dust pan. It gets five times as much as a little fireplace shovel.

Hauling your ashes
Use a metal bucket for removing ashes. Even overnight after a fire, there can still be live embers hidden in the ashes. If you use a paper bag, the embers could liven things up while the bag sits on the back porch.

To keep from having airborne ashes floating throughout the house, lightly mist the ashes with water before you start scooping them up.

Cover the filled ash bucket with wet newspapers to hold 'em down as you carry them out.

Ashes aren't trash

Use the ashes on icy walks and drives for better traction.

If the soil conditions are right, ashes from the fireplace can be spread around plants or mixed with dirt or the compost heap with good results. Check with your nurseryman first!

A nifty patch

Old timers made their own patching compound from two parts ashes, one part salt, and enough water to make it into a thick paste.

ENERGY SAVERS

Insulation

Up in the attic

If your attic has loose-fill insulation that needs to be leveled, make an insulation spreading tool by stretching a wide rubber band from an old inner tube over the fingers of a yard rake.

Or, just turn the rake over and use the back to spread.

When handling fiberglass insulation, the fibers can cut your hands. Wear rubber or leather gloves to protect yourself.

It's a good idea to wear a mask to prevent inhaling any of the insulation fibers.

Also wear your hard hat because shingle nails are often sticking down that can pierce your head.

Hedge clippers do a good job cutting batts of insulation.

Rigid foam covered with fabric can be cut to fit and be wedged into window frames to keep out the cold. Keep these panels stored under the bed when not needed over the windows.

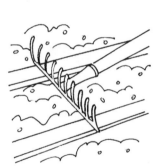

Back of rake distributes loose-fill insulation.

Too much heat

Insulation in the attic should not cover up recessed lighting fixtures. The trapped heat could start a house fire. A barrier can be made from a two-pound coffee can with both ends cut out or from a larger can.

Unusual insulation
A floor-to-ceiling bookshelf on a north wall is great insulation.

Don't forget
Lots of energy loss can occur around a medicine cabinet. The wall cavity can act as a chimney for air drafts. Pack insulation around the unit and stop the loss.

Weatherstripping

More holding power
Peel-and-stick weatherstripping will adhere better to a clean surface that's been lightly sanded.

It also helps to run a hand-held hair dryer over the surface to warm it.

The leak locator
One of the best ways to find where a window or door has air leaks is to use a hand-held hair dryer outside and have a friend dampen the back of the hand and follow you as you go around the crack. At places where air is coming in, the damp hand will feel cooler.

Caulking

Temperature control
When using caulk during cold weather wrap the cartridge with a heating pad. When warm, caulk flows out much easier.

The reverse can be true in summer. If the caulk is too runny, put it in the refrigerator for a spell.

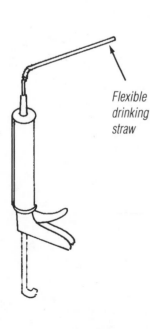

Flexible drinking straw

Smoother
If a bead of caulk doesn't look all that great, smooth it with a damp finger.

Reach out
To get caulk into hard-to-reach places, slip a large flexible drinking straw into the spout. Tape it in place.

The capper
If there's still caulk left after you're through, use a wire

nut, an electrical wire splicing device, over the spout. The threads inside bite into the plastic spout.

Or, use a sheet metal screw, the threads of which bite into the inside of the spout.

Semi-free Heat for Winter

Won't drain your bank account
Instead of sending still warm bath water down the drain, let it cool to add heat to the house.

Not just a lot of hot air
Keep heat from the electric clothes dryer in by exhausting into the house instead of outside. To keep the lint from going into the house, cover the exhaust with an old nylon stocking.

Open the dishwasher at the end of the cycle and lots of warm air will come into the room

Join the fan club
Your ceiling fan set on reverse can recycle hot air that rises. Use a slow speed. This is particularly good with high ceilings.

What's cooking?
When cooking, adjust the thermostat down a tad. The heat from cooking will make up the difference.

Party time
About half an hour before the guests arrive, cut back on heating as the warm bodies will keep the party hot, hot, hot!

Hats and hugs
Quite a bit of body heat escapes through your head. Wearing a hat keeps that heat in.

Two shivering humans can hug and both feel warmer. It costs nothing and is fun.

Plumbing and Electrical Tips

PLUMBING

Pipes

Noisy pipes
Many times you have noises because pipes move from the force of the water. Slip a slit section of garden hose over the pipe and anchor it with a pipe clamp.

    Pipe straps hold long runs of pipe up to prevent sagging. If you don't have any, make your own by spiral cutting a strip from a plastic bleach bottle.

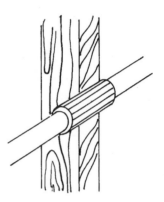

Slit garden hose cushions vibrating pipe.

Leaks

Water, water everywhere
You must shut off the water supply to the area where the leak is. If there is no shutoff valve for that area, there usually is a main shutoff and one at the meter. Test these now while there's no problem to be sure they work.

Cut here

Tag with instructions
The bottom of a bleach bottle is a good tag for the shut-off. Label it with waterproof ink and also include arrows showing the direction for "off" and "on."

The quick way
Epoxy glue can handle the pressure on a water supply line. Be sure to give it ample time to set up before that pressure is returned to the line with the leak.

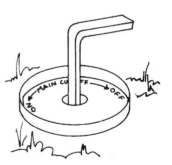

Another way
Place a pad of rubber from an old inner tube over the leak and use a worm-gear hose clamp to hold it tight enough to stop the leak.

A hole in one?
If you've poked a hole in an underground plastic pipe, rather than cut out the bad part, at least try this. Grate up some PVC from a pipe scrap and mix it into the PVC adhesive and quickly smear this paste onto the clean dry pipe. It may work!

A sweat soldering tip
When you work on copper pipes, use the process called sweat soldering. If there is water still in the pipe, the soldered joint may fail. A rolled up ball of fresh bread can be poked into the pipe about an inch or so. This dries the area and keeps the water back. After the repair the water will come through and dissolve the bread and send it out through a faucet.

Gaining access
Sometimes you must cut into a wall to work on plumbing. If you'd like to have permanent access to a shower or tub, cover the opening with a heating system return air vent. It looks good.

Or, hold a wooden panel in place with magnetic cabinet catches.

Drips

Don't eat the chrome
Before gripping a chrome part to remove a faucet for repair, wrap a rag or masking tape around to protect the finish.

Or, use a strip of rubber from an old inner tube.

Sleep tight!
Until you can replace a washer for a proper repair, put a sponge under the drip at night to make it less noisy.

Back in the wall
To remove a shower faucet in a tile wall, you may need a special socket wrench to reach the nut. You may have a socket the proper size but with the faucet stem sticking out, the wrench can't work the socket. No problem. Use a pipe wrench to turn the socket.

Outsmarting Jack Frost

To avoid frozen pipes, leave all faucets open to allow for a steady drip. Moving water is less likely to freeze.

Open kitchen and bath cabinets to allow warmer air from the room to help keep the pipes warm.

Hang a large light bulb under sinks for additional heat. If you use a space heater, be sure it's a safe distance from anything combustible.

Too late?

If pipes are frozen, open the taps so that when thawing does occur, the pressure has an escape out the faucet rather than bursting the pipe.

Start the thawing process as close to the faucet as possible and work backward from it.

A hand-held air dryer or a heat lamp are slow but safe ways to thaw a frozen pipe.

Clogged Drains

The plumber's friend

When using a plumber, be sure all other openings, such as the other side of a double sink or the overflow in a lavatory, are covered so the force goes on down the drain.

Smear shortening or petroleum jelly around the lip of the plunger for a better seal.

If the handle keeps coming loose, a worm-gear hose clamp around the top of the rubber cup will make it stay in place.

Half of a large hollow rubber ball may provide enough force to remove a little clog.

Snake to the rescue

The plumber's snake can break up clogs but is always going to come out very messy. Coil it into a plastic trash bag and contain the mess . . . and the snake.

Or, coil it into a big plastic bucket or small plastic garbage can. Even a corrugated box can tame the snake.

The homemade drain formula

Make you own inexpensive kitchen drain cleaner by combining:

1 cup baking soda
1 cup table salt
$^1/_4$ cup cream of tartar

Mix well, Use only $^1/_4$ cup of the mix directly down the drain followed by two cups of boiling water. After a minute, flush with tap water. This is not for a completely clogged drain but, done weekly, it's good preventive maintenance and keeps the kitchen sink trap grease-free and good smelling.

More preventive maintenance

Washing soda, not to be confused with baking soda, is a good preventive maintenance drain cleaner. Put a half cup directly down the drain and slowly pour two quarts of hot water to follow. Do this weekly to avoid clogs.

Lots of folks pour a pot of boiling water down the drain about once a week and never have a clog problem. Be careful not to scald yourself.

Boiling vinegar does an even better job.

Chemical drain openers ☠

Use a big plastic funnel in the drain opening so the chemicals don't get on the chrome or sink.

Never mix two different brands of drain cleaner. The chemicals could have a violent reaction.

For a kitchen sink clog, pour a box of soda down the drain and then pour in a pint of vinegar. It will often move clogs out of the sink trap.

Low Water Pressure

Flush out the guck

In an older home, low water pressure is often from mineral deposits in the lines. Turn off the entire system at the main shutoff. Then open the tap that is the farthest away from the main shutoff. When you turn the water supply back on, the force of the water can force lots of the deposits out the open tap.

The aerator

Often low pressure at one faucet is because the aerator is clogged. Remove and clean before you call for help.

ELECTRICAL

Safety

The entry box ⚡

When working on a circuit, don't rely on the wall switch being off. Go to the entry box or fuse box and trip the circuit breaker or remove the fuse to that circuit.

Don't become a conductor ⚡

When at the entry box, stand on a 2x4 or wooden platform and wear rubber-soled shoes.

Touch the entry box with only one hand. (Wise old electricians put the other hand in a pocket.)

Never use a metal ladder when doing electrical work.

Is this the right switch? ⚡

If you don't have a helper, plug a radio into the circuit you want to shut off and when you trip the right breaker you'll hear the silence.

Or, that whining old vacuum cleaner can also tell you if it's the right one.

Hands off! ⚡

When you leave the entry box to work, put a large sign on the box to warn others that work is being done and no switches are to be touched.

Confused about fuses? ⚡

Never replace a fuse with one of a different amperage than the one removed.

Bugs in the box?

Insects, including wasps, have been known to nest in fuse boxes. If there's room for this to happen, a few mothballs will keep the unwelcome guests out.

An annual trip ⚡

Once a year, it's a good idea to trip and reset all circuit breaker switches. Any corrosion can cause it not to trip in an emergency.

Lighten up

Keep a flashlight with a magnet to hold it in place against the circuit breaker box.

Shrinking the possibility of shock 🔌

By slipping shrink tubing up on the shank of a screw-driver, it's safer against touching the wrong thing.

Tester trick

Store your circuit tester in a slit tennis ball for protection. Just crimp the ball to open it up.

Bulbs

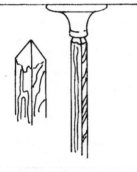

Pointed stick removes broken bulb.

Can't even change a light bulb? 🔌

A broken bulb can be a hassle to remove. With the current off, jam a sponge rubber ball into the broken bulb. It'll catch the sharp parts and you can twist the bulb out. Remember, turn counterclockwise to remove.

Or, use a fresh, firm, uncooked baking potato cut in half. (The potato won't taste all that good afterwards.)

With gloves on, use a wadded newspaper to remove the broken bulb.

Give a point to a 2x2 stick and force it into the bulb.

A rolled up magazine can also be jammed into the broken bulb for removal.

The best way is to grab the bulb's base with needle nose pliers. Once again, *be sure the current is off!*

Lamps

The new lamp cord ploy

Rather than trying to feed new wiring through a lamp base, tape the new wire to the old and as you pull the old wire out, the new wire follows it in.

Wiring

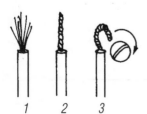

1   2   3

The right curl 🔌

When attaching wiring to a switch or wall outlet, curl the end to fit around the screw in a clockwise fashion. That way, as the screw is tightened, the wire is pulled tighter under the screw for a better connection.

Extension Cords

Storage
The cardboard cylinder from a roll of paper towels is a good holder of small extension cords.

Or, use a length of PVC plumbing pipe for larger cords.

Here's a tricky holder for cord. Cut two slits in a gallon plastic jug, one near the top and another near the bottom. Make them just a tad smaller than the cord. Slip one end in a slit and wind the cord around the jug. When fully wound, slip the other end in the other slot. The holder can hang by its handle when not in use.

A bucket of juice
Cut a hole in a plastic pail big enough to feed an extension cord plug through and then coil the cord in the bucket. You have a tangle-free cord with an easy-to-carry tote.

The long and short of it
It's a shame to have to use a fifty-foot cord when you only need a few extra feet. Any time you damage an extension cord, it's an opportunity to make it into one or more shorter cords. Get the plugs needed and then make four-, six-, or eight-foot cords. You'll find them very useful.

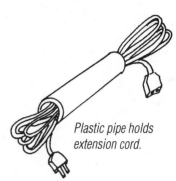

Plastic pipe holds extension cord.

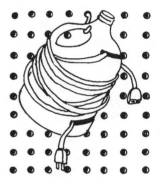

Jug cord holder

Painting and Wallpapering

PAINTING

Color Selection

Color magic
Use color to create illusions. Light colors tend to make a
room look larger.

A bowling alley-like room will look wider if you use
pastel colors on three walls and a bright color on one
short wall.

A low ceiling can be "raised" by painting it a lighter
color than the walls.

If you have a too-big piece of furniture or an ugly
radiator, make it blend into the background by painting it
the same color as the walls.

Think big!
Trying to select the right color from one of those tiny
paint chips often doesn't work. Buy a pint and roll it on
the wall. It can be covered over if not right.

Some folks prefer to paint a piece of poster board to
tape to the wall.

A buying trick
When buying the paint, be sure to get enough cans and be
sure that they are from the same batch number.

For the record
Put a strip of tape on the back of a light switch plate with
the color and amount used for each room written on it.

Preparation and Protection

A lead alert 🖼
In an older home there's liable to be lead-based paint. Be sure to wear a proper respirator.

No paint tray clean-up
Line the paint roller tray with plastic from a dry cleaner bag. When the paint job is done, peel away the plastic and throw it away. The tray is still clean!

Or use aluminum foil the same way.

No back flips
With very slick floors, use a canvas drop cloth. Plastic drop cloths and newspapers can slide right out from under you.

Protect the floors
Put a coat of wax over floors before painting. Any drips will come up when you buff after painting.

Here's paint in your eye 🖼
When painting a ceiling, wear glasses to prevent paint droplets from getting into your eyes.

A swim mask can also come to your rescue.

No spots before your eyes
If you wear glasses, cover each lens with a patch of clear plastic wrap. When the chore is done, peel away the plastic and you won't see spots before your eyes.

Fuchsia hair among the gold
Wear a shower cap to protect your hair.

Or, make a hat from a paper bag.

If you get paint in your hair, washerless hand cleaner from the shop will help. Apply, and after about thirty minutes, the paint slides right off.

A handy idea
A pair of rubber gloves that have sprung a leak can still be good painting gloves to keep paint off your hands.

Slip a plastic sandwich bag over your hands if you leave the paint area. This protects door knobs and other things from paint prints.

Don't trash your clothes with paint
Even old clothes deserve some protection. Make a smock from a trash bag by cutting holes for your arms and head.

Don't sweat out your shoe shine
A pair of stretched-out old sweat socks can be pulled over your sneakers. Not only do they protect the footwear but if you drip, you can do a quick wipe-up with your foot.

Or, slip a plastic bag over each foot.

Protect your hide
You can protect your skin by applying cold cream to your face. When you wipe it away, any paint you spattered will not have gotten on your skin.

Petroleum jelly does the same thing.

Time marches on
If you have a time fetish and must know what time it is during your paint job, wrap your wrist watch with clear plastic wrap. The wrap takes all the paint dribbles but you can still see what time it is.

A diet for painted hands
Salad dressing rubbed into the skin removes paint. Of course, your cat could mistake you for a snack.

A free hand cleaner
Work bacon grease or some other drained cooking grease over your hands to remove paint.

Bag the lights
Cover light fixtures with plastic trash bags taped in place.

Plastic bag protects light fixture.

Protection for furniture
If you can't remove the furniture, at least give it a coat of paste wax, but don't buff. Any spatters of paint will probably buff away, but if not, when you strip the wax the paint will go, too.

If paint drips on a waxed piece that has been buffed, use a hair dryer to melt the wax and both wax and paint can be wiped up. Then rewax the spot.

Wall cleaning formula
Here's a good prepainting wall cleaner. Mix one part

baking soda, one part white vinegar, and two parts house-hold ammonia. Scrub and rinse.

Start at the bottom
When washing walls, start at the bottom and work up. Otherwise, dirty water will run down a dirty wall and cause streaks.

Water spots
Lots of folks think a coat of paint will do away with water spots on the ceiling, but they nearly always bleed through. Seal them with clear shellac or one of the products made for this.

Or, paint over the spots with evaporated milk — the kind that comes in the little cans.

Masking

Lip tip
Run chapstick around glass instead of masking. Wipe away paint after you've finished.

Old news
Cut newspaper the size of the panes. Wet it and it'll stay in place long enough to paint around it.

A moving masker
For masking the floor when painting the baseboards, a large venetian blind slat will fit under the molding and move along as you paint.

Or, you can use a shirt board.

A non-stick trick
You know how a newly painted object always sticks to the newspaper underneath? It won't happen if you'll use wax paper instead.

Even a bread wrapper will do.

The bumper sticker trick
Collect bumper stickers to use when wider masking is needed.

For curvy areas, make a pattern of paper and then transfer to the bumper stickers.

Mixing

What's the name of that color?

Before opening the can, write the name and number of the color on the bottom of the can. That way it can't get covered with drips in case you need to get more of the same.

Nailing down the mess

If you use a nail to tap in a series of holes all around the rim of the can, the paint that fills in the rim will drip back down into the can and not squish out when it comes time to put the lid back on.

Mixing technique

It's best to pour off about one-third of the paint from a new can into a second container. Stir the first can and then mix them together by pouring back and forth.

Non-slosh

If you try to stir a full can of paint, some will slosh out. Add to the height of the can by wrapping a section of newspaper around the can. It can be held by tape. By pulling it up, you have, in effect, raised the height of the can so any splashing gets on the paper.

Cardboard guides paint.

No poor pouring

For neater pouring, curve a shirt board and stick it into the paint. Pour slowly. Now the paint completely misses the rim for a much neater pour.

Avoid pouring altogether and use a soup ladle to transfer paint.

Automatic mixing ⚡

Never use a mixing attachment in your electric drill when stirring solvent-based coatings. Arcing in the drill motor could be enough of a start to launch you into outer space.

Insert the shaft of a stirring attachment through the center of a paper plate before chucking it into the drill. With the plate snug down against the can, there's no chance of splattering.

Or, keep a paint can lid with a hole in the center and install this on the can before stirring.

A beater blade from the kitchen mixer does a good paint mixing job in a power drill.

Oil paint can lid with hole for mixing.

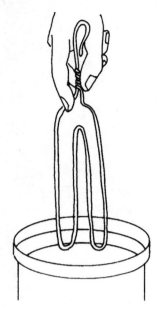

Teflon-coated plastic spoon or spatula with holes drilled becomes paint stirrer.

Or, if you don't mind doing it by hand, an old egg beater works fine.

Make a mixer
Bend a wire coat hanger so the two ends are almost straight down and you have a super paint stirrer.

The mixed-up marbles
Just before sealing up leftover paint, toss in a few marbles so all you have to do to mix next time is shake 'em up.

No strain straining
If a paint skin develops, strain it by pouring through a nylon stocking.

To hold the stocking in place, use a plastic lid on a two-pound coffee can but cut away all but the lip of the lid. Snapped in place over the can and nylon, it'll hold the stocking.

Or, use a large tea strainer to pour through.

Automatic strainer
Rather than straining, cut a circle of screen wire and put it in the paint can. As it sinks, it carries skin to the bottom.

Something from the kitchen
Teflon-coated spoons and spatulas are super stirring tools. Drill some holes in these tools and they're even better.

Applying the Paint

Paint party
If you have an entire house to paint, invite some friends and have a paint party. However, no goodies until the job is done.

A box of paint trays
Extra people mean you need extra paint roller trays. A large cereal box lined with foil or plastic will work well.

How far to go?
Never take a break in the middle of a wall. When you come back and paint against a dry edge, it'll usually show.

Also, never open a new can of paint in the middle of the wall. You can usually see a slight difference.

A drip catcher
Glue a paper plate to the bottom of the can to collect the drips.

Paper plate glued to can

For the second time around
For the second coat, draw three wavy horizontal lines over the wall with a pencil. Then if you have skips, you'll see them.

Big time paint tray
With a large paint job, a roll-around commercial mop bucket can replace the roller tray. Lean a regular tray-grid into the bucket.

Tray on wheels
Put the paint tray in a kid's wagon and roll it to the paint site. You won't have to bend over as far to load your roller.

Hang on to those buckets
A strong wooden coat hanger will allow you to carry three paint buckets at once.

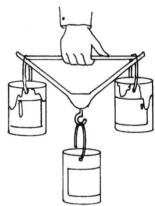

No tip-over
Use a bunge cord to hook under the paint shelf of your ladder to hold the bucket in place.

You won't cry over spilled paint
To ensure the bucket can't fall off, install a large C-clamp to the top step of the ladder and anchor the can to it with a big rubber band.

To avoid a tipped paint can, cut a hole in the side of a big detergent or cereal box to fit the can. This also catches the drips.

Make two slits to form an "X" in the bottom of a plastic bottle bottom and insert a small paint can in to prevent tip-over.

Paint mitt
For painting railings and the like, slip a plastic bag over your hand and then cover that with an old sweat sock. Dip your hand in the paint and grab the railing and move

Bottom of 2-liter pop bottle

up and down. Much faster than with a brush. When the job is done, toss the sock and remove the bag to see a clean hand.

A cup of paint
A pint can of paint will fit into a coffee mug. You've now got a handle for less mess.

A brush tote
Cut the top half off a two-liter soft drink bottle, add two slits for your belt, and you have a handy holster for when you must put the brush down for a moment.

A brush holster
Tape a foil-lined food pouch to the paint can as a brush holder.

Roller holder
If you're using a roller with an extension handle and want to take a break, one of those orange or yellow traffic cones will help you out. Just poke the handle into the opening and the roller is held upright and can't touch anything to make a mess.

Bed of nails
To paint small objects, try a bed of nails. Poke lots of nails through a corrugated board. The points will hold the object and there will be no problem of sticking as there might be with newspaper underneath.

It's done with mirrors
When painting in cabinets, use a mirror to let you see the bottom of the bottom shelf.

Door edges
When going from one room to another where two colors are involved, paint the door edge to match the color in the room into which it opens.

Particle board
The edges of particle board are very porous. To prevent their drinking up the paint or finish, coat the edges with thinned shellac.

You can also use white glue.

Painting silicone

Most silicone sealant won't accept paint. But the sealant will accept contact adhesive and that will accept paint.

Or, use an artist's fixative available at art supply stores.

Shutters are easy

Shutters are easier to paint if you'll install a pair of screw eyes to the bottom edge and hang them from the clothesline. You can spray all surfaces without having to handle the shutter.

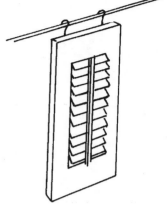

A topshelf idea

Drive two nails part way in each end of a shelf and you won't have to wait until the first side dries to paint the other. The nails rest on a pair of sawhorses and you can flip the shelf without touching anything but the nails.

Painting pots

Run a cord through the hole in a clay pot with a knot inside to let you hang it upside down for easy all-over painting without touching the pot.

Radiators

When it's time to paint the radiators, let them heat up a bit and then apply the paint while the metal is warm. The paint will adhere better.

Staple a sponge to a yardstick to paint the back side of the radiator.

Clean Up Your Act

Paint on your skin?

When you get paint on your skin, try a little shaving cream for quick removal.

Or, try cooking oil.

Sawdust soaked in turpentine is an excellent hand cleaner for painters.

Paint on your clothes?

Equal parts of turpentine and ammonia may remove spots from fabric.

Brush cleaning in a bag
For neater brush cleaning, put the brush in a plastic bag, pour in the solvent, and seal the bag around the handle with rubber bands.

The sling thing
Removing solvent from a brush is usually done by fast arm motion that slings it out. This can be a mess. Not if you put it in a grocery bag while holding the handle and the top of the bag. All of the mess stays in the bag.

A hot tip
Remove several layers of paint from a metal roller tray with a propane torch.

A coin trick
If your masking didn't work and you got paint on the window pane, use a copper penny as a scraper. It works and you won't cut your finger as you might with a razor blade.

Storage for Leftovers

For touch-ups
Pour a little of the leftover paint into a cleaned shoe polish bottle of the type that has a dauber brush in the cap. It's ideal for quick touch-ups.

Or, use a plastic dust pan and a paint pad for touch-ups. The pan holds the paint and the pad makes a less visible touch-up. Both are easy to clean.

No squishing
Before tapping the lid down tight, cover the can with a plastic garment bag to catch any paint squished out.

Or, put the can and lid in a bag before tapping it closed.

The inside story
You can tell you much of what color is in the can if you paint a line on the side of the can to indicate the level.

Leftover storage
Put a plastic bag into an empty can and pour leftovers

into the bag. Then work the air out as you seal the bag. No air, no skin!

Or, run rubber cement around the lip of the lid for a more airtight seal.

Place a strip of clear plastic wrap over the top of the can for a better seal when the lid is tapped into place.

No air, no paint skin

Just before closing the can, exhale into the can. Your breath has no oxygen and will expel the air in the can. (If it changes the color of the paint, you better see your dentist.)

Leftovers

Before opening leftover paint that won't all be used, mark a line on the lid and down the side of the can. When you replace the lid, line the marks up. Otherwise the paint in the rim and on the lid might prevent your getting a good seal.

Aerosol painting

After you've finished spraying, turn the can upside down and push the button. This clears all paint from the tube and the tip so it's ready to go the next time.

A paint booth

Spraying shoots paint out that could go all over everything and that's why a booth is so necessary. A big corrugated appliance carton is super and it's free.

Maybe you like the idea of using your fireplace as a booth. Fumes and odors go up the chimney and paint flecks will burn off. Be sure there aren't any ashes to be stirred up to botch your paint job.

A Brush-up on Brushes and Rollers

Take five

If you need to take a break, wrap your roller or brush in plastic and stick it in the refrigerator. It'll be ready to go when you are.

Get the same deal with aluminum foil.

Rub-a-dub-dub

An old-timey washboard is an excellent surface against

which you can work paint from a brush. Have a container below to catch and reuse the solvent as it runs off. For latex, use soap and water.

A prince of an idea
A frog, used to hold cut flowers in a vase, can be put into a can of solvent to work the brush against.

Tiny brush care
Poke a tiny artist's brush into a drinking straw to protect it in storage.

An ace of a roller tip
Soak a roller in a tennis ball can. Since it's almost an exact fit, it uses less solvent.
    Or, use a quart milk carton.

"X" cut holds brush at right level in solvent.

X-pert brush soaker
Make an "X" slit in a plastic coffee can lid, push the brush handle through, and soak the brush in the can — the "X" will hold it up so the bristles don't touch bottom. Also, there's no evaporation.

Solving solvent loss
Reclaim solvent after soaking brushes by waiting a few days. The paint will have settled to the bottom of the container. Pour slowly and the solvent you pour off will be clean and pure.

Shape up
Reshape a brush by dipping it in white water-soluble glue. Let the glue dry and the brush will hold its shape. Wash out the glue when you need the brush.

De-bug your brushes
Did you know that moths will eat the bristles of a natural bristle brush? When you wrap the brush, include moth crystals to keep 'em away. Nylon brushes attract only synthetic moths.

Make a touch-up brush
A small tab of foam rubber upholstery plus a spring-type clothespin will make a fine touch-up brush. Trash the pad when you're through.

WALLPAPERING

Preparation

A work table
Wallpapering requires quite a bit of space. Remove a slab door, take off the hardware and you have a great table. The wallpaper paste will wash off after the job is done.

Or, put a 4x8 sheet of plywood across a bed.

If papering in the bath, cut plywood to fit over the tub.

Smart buying
Be sure to order enough paper before you start and make certain all rolls are from the same run. Otherwise there may be a slight difference in colors.

Preparing the Wall

Smoothing the way
Rather than sanding off the bumps of a textured wall, use drywall compound and a metal float (a concrete smoothing tool) to add a new smooth surface to the wall.

The brick trick
A smooth brick is a good tool to smooth a textured wall.

If you do sand 🔦 🗔
Hang plastic vapor barrier material over all doors leading out of the area in which you're sanding. This way no sanding dust can float throughout the house. Open a window in that room to let dust escape.

A dampened bedsheet will block the door and also catch the dust.

Off with the old!
Use very hot water to remove old wallpaper. Add a little liquid detergent to the water to help it soak through.

One of the best applicators for the water is a paint roller.

Or, try a sponge mop.

A pump-up sprayer can mist the water over the old surface.

You can press sections of wet newspaper against the wall and it will soak through.

Power peeling
A power roller that pumps paint through a tube to the roller will do the same with sudsy hot water for wallpaper stripping.

If you have vinyl paper, water won't penetrate. Use a utility knife and make slits over the surface so water can get in.

Or, rake a saw across the surface with the teeth pushed firmly against the wall so that penetration is made.

The same is true for painted paper.

Picture this
If you wish to get wall hangings back in the same spot, stick a toothpick in the nail hole. As you apply the paper, let the toothpicks stab through.

Getting the Hang of It

Old paperhanger's trick
Before the newer pastes came along, old-timers put a pinch each of alum and salt into the paste. If you're using regular wheat paste, try it. This will make the paste adhere better and give you a smoother wall covering.

Avoid skips
Add a few drops of blue cake coloring to the paste. The faint blue tint lets you see if you've missed any spots.

Speedy paster
A paint roller is a fast way to apply paste. You can also mix the paste in a roller tray for even faster work.

Smooth ceiling
A broom does a good job of smoothing ceiling paper from ground level.

Or, use a paint pad with an extension handle.

A saving idea
With some patterns, you use less paper by alternating rolls to match. At $40 a roll it can make a difference.

Play it safe

Those little pieces with wet paste that you trim off are as treacherous as a banana peel if you step on 'em wrong. Fold them paste-to-paste so you don't end up doing a half gainer.

Repairing Goofs

Bubble, bubble, that's the trouble

If, after a few days, you notice a bubble in one of the panels, press it lightly. If it feels like there is still active paste inside, try making a pinhole to release the paste.

Another solution: make two cuts to form an "X." Fold the flaps back and work air or paste out. Then use an artist's brush to add new paste to glue down the flaps.

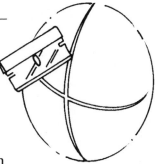

Slit "X" to repair wallpaper bubble.

Patch technique

Tear a patch from a scrap so that the underside has a feathered edge. This can give you an almost invisible patch.

Save the paste

After you've finished a papering job, fill a small plastic bottle with the paste for repairs.

If you discover loose seams and don't have any leftover paste, mashed potatoes will do the job.

Spot removers

Use an art gum eraser or kneaded eraser to gently remove many spots from wallpaper.

Or, try a rolled up wad of soft rye bread.

Talcum powder will take away oily hand prints around light switches.

See spot leave

Or, dip a dry cloth into dry borax powder.

Furniture Care

GENERAL FURNITURE CLEANING

More about waxy buildup ⑥

The most common cause of grime on furniture is old waxy buildup. Paint thinner on a rag will remove old wax without damage to the finish.

> Here's a furniture cleaning formula you can make:
> 3 parts boiled linseed oil (You do not boil the linseed oil. That's what you ask for.)
> 2 parts turpentine
> 1 part white vinegar

> Use this on a well-wrung-out rag. The mix will work better if it's warm—but do not heat over a flame. Heat a pan of water and then remove if from the stove. Put a smaller container of the mix into the hot water. Wipe this on and then wipe it off. Then buff well.

Chewing gum

Chewing gum left under furniture can often be softened for scraping with aerosol shaving cream.

Care for your wood

In winter when the house is dry, wax the unfinished underside of pieces to prevent the wood from drying out.

Surface Damage

Scratches and gouges

Hide minor scratches with one of these tricks:
> Apply paste wax and buff to a shine.
> Take a nut meat from a pecan or walnut, break it in

half, and rub along each scratch. The oil from the nut will hide many scratches.

Peanut butter will hide many scratches.

Iodine matches some stains.

Crayons come in many different shades. If you find a match, it will also leave a shine on the surface.

Liquid shoe polish may do the job.

One teaspoon of instant coffee in two spoons of water makes an excellent scratch hider for dark wood furniture. Use a little less coffee for lighter pieces.

Other folks prefer to dissolve the coffee in salad oil.

Scratch proofing

Cut tiny rubber wafers from a pencil eraser to glue to the bottom of items that might scratch the furniture.

Or, cut disks from an old felt hat.

Burn marks

Use a dull knife to scrape away the charred matter. If that takes you into the wood, you may have to add stain. Then bring it up to level with the rest of the surface with clear fingernail polish thinned half and half with polish remover. Apply in thin coats, letting each dry before applying the next.

Water spots?

A mild abrasive plus a lubricant will remove water marks. Squeeze out toothpaste and rub with a damp rag wrapped around your finger.

Ashes, baking soda, salt, or fine steel wool are other alternatives.

Use mayonnaise or cooking oil as a lubricant.

Mayonnaise and heat from a hair dryer will often do the job.

Rub with cooking oil and loose tobacco from a cigarette.

Or, rub with peanut butter.

Petroleum jelly and a pencil eraser will do it.

If you don't like rubbing, just cover the water spot with petroleum jelly and leave overnight. When you wipe away the jelly, the spot will be gone, too.

An old waiter's trick

A pat of butter in a cloth napkin will rub away a water spot.

FURNITURE REPAIRS

Loose casters

You can often stop a loose caster from falling out of a
furniture leg by wrapping the stem with steel wood before
reinserting.

Or, saw a slit in the top of the stem using a hacksaw.
Then spread it apart with a screwdriver and it will stay in
place.

Loose joints

Use a hypodermic needle to inject wood glue into the
joints of loose chair rungs. Saves taking the entire chair
apart.

Wrap a thin sliver of wood shaving around a rung
before gluing to take up the gap.

A strip from a nylon stocking also takes up the gap.

Or, wrap the end of the rung with thread.

Make a wedge from a piece of a clothespin and insert
it into a slot cut in
the rung. When pushed into place, this will spread the
rung to make for a tight fit.

While glue will often take up a gap, thicken it with
sawdust and be sure.

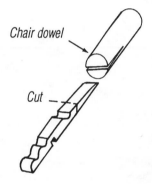

Chair dowel

Cut

Broken parts

If using dowels to repair furniture, heat the dowels in the
oven to remove all moisture. When the dowels are in
place, they pick up moisture from the air and expand.

Round off the ends of dowels on a bench grinder to
create reservoirs for the glue.

Veneer

With bubbles, dampen the surface to make the veneer
flexible, then drill a tiny hole and inject glue with a syr-
inge. Use weights to clamp.

For chipped edges, use the side of a soft lead pencil
rubbed back and forth over a sheet of paper to transfer
pattern of missing veneer.

REFINISHING

A strip joint

Always open a can of paint and varnish remover slowly to

release the pressure that builds up in many such products. Otherwise it could blast out and get on you.

Use old or cheap brushes for applying stripper.

Brush only one way, never back and forth, as that disturbs the protective coating that retards evaporation.

When stripping a table or chair, put flat tuna cans under the legs to catch the drips. This makes for less mess and the stripper in the cans is reusable.

Cover the stripper with plastic sheeting, such as a dry cleaner bag or trash bag: evaporation is retarded so that the stripper keeps working longer.

Scraping

A handful of sawdust spread over the stripper makes it neater and easier when it comes time to scrape away the sludge.

An expired credit card makes a good scraper.

Or, try a stiff scrub brush.

The sludge is easily handled if you scrape it into a plastic dust pan. It's lightweight and the stuff goes right out into the garbage can.

A Teflon spatula is stiff enough to remove the sludge and is bigger than a putty knife but will never scratch the wood.

Spritz some of that no-stick cooking oil spray on your scraper and the sludge from the stripper won't stick.

To remove paint down in grooves on a turned furniture leg, dip a length of string into the stripper and then work the string back and forth in the groove. The string gets the stripper into the groove and then scrapes away the paint.

Or, twist a nylon stocking until ropelike.

A nut pick or even toothpicks may also help in the removal.

So that you don't get steel slivers in your hands, poke steel wool into a rubber chair tip as a handle.

Or, use an empty shotgun shell.

Bleaching

Regular laundry bleach will remove most spots from wood after the finish has been stripped.

Put the piece in the sun and the warmed wood will bleach faster.

Or, use a hand-held hair dryer for warming the spot.

Staining

Here's my old grandpappy's formula for tobacco stain:

> 1 plug chewing tobacco
> 1 pint household ammonia

Crumble the tobacco into a quart jar and pour the ammonia over it. Seal it tightly for 10 days. Open it outside as it has a strong odor. Strain it and apply to unfinished furniture with a soft cloth. It's a real conversation piece!

Perk up your furniture

Another stain you can make is with coffee grounds. Store the wet grounds in a tightly sealed jar. When it's full, drain off the liquid and let it simmer. What's left is a beautiful stain.

Gaze into the future

To see if the wood needs stain, apply paint thinner to about a foot square section with a rag. While wet, it will look very much like a clear finish will. Better than a crystal ball!

Painting

You don't need to strip furniture for painting. Just clean and remove the gloss from the old finish.

If you are spray painting a piece of furniture, use a large corrugated appliance crate as a spray booth to contain the spray.

Put wax paper or foil under the legs to prevent the paint from sticking to the newspapers.

Or, stick a tack or nail partway into each leg.

A flattened milk carton under the piece will also protect the carpet.

Finishing

When using varnish, never shake the can to mix. Shaking creates bubbles that will end up as part of the finish.

Varnish is slow to dry and, while wet, any airborne dust will stick in the varnish. So use it in a dust-free room.

If you have central air, turn off the fan for an hour before starting.

Wear lint-free clothing.

As you apply varnish or any other clear finish, have a light source on the other side of the furniture. The reflection will let you know if you skipped any spots.

An appetizing finish

Experiment with a mix of two parts boiled linseed oil, one part turpentine, and one part polyurethane as a furniture finish. Bet you'll like it.

Antiquing

Old furniture shows its age. To make a new piece look like an antique use a rasp, file, or sandpaper to round off all edges and corners to simulate years of handlings.

Worm holes can be made with an ice pick.

Give the piece real character by beating it with chains, keys, or other objects. But don't get carried away.

Most antiquing kits have a glaze that goes over a base coat. Make your own glaze by adding thinned artist's oil paints to clear varnish.

Or, thin the varnish with up to three parts turpentine before squeezing in the color.

Lint picker-upper

A tack rag will pick up lint before you start to varnish. Here's how to make your own. Start with a much-laundered, lint-free cotton cloth. Diapers are great. Dip in warm water and wring out. Dip in turpentine and wring. Drip varnish over it and fold back and forth to completely coat. It should be tacky enough to pick up dust without leaving any varnish.

Store your tack rag in a tightly sealed jar.

Restore a dry tack rag with drips of water and turpentine.

Suck it up!

A vacuum cleaner will get most dust before you varnish.

Confucius says . . .

Pick up stray brush hairs with toothpicks, sort of in the manner you use chopsticks.

A hot idea

For a different finish, use a propane torch over bare wood. Keep it moving! The charred look can be waxed for protection. Experiment first on a scrap.

Stenciling

Old X-ray film is excellent stencil paper.

Waxing

Auto paste wax will probably give a harder finish than the furniture wax you're now using.

Warm up the wood with a hair dryer before waxing. You'll have easier application and deeper penetration.

Or, warm the cloth in your dryer before applying furniture wax.

Polishing

A lamb's-wool shoe brush is a super polisher for furniture.

Make your own polish with one part vinegar and three parts olive oil.

Or, make lemon oil furniture polish by adding five drops of lemon extract to a pint of mineral oil.

Polish lacquer by making a paste of cornstarch and olive oil. Rub in and then buff to the desired shine.

After applying a new finish, give the piece a final polishing with a plain sheet of typing paper and a little oil.

Extend your pure oil polishes with less expensive equal parts of turpentine.

Upholstery

Store leftover fabric scraps in a large envelope stapled to the bottom of the piece.

When installing upholstery tacks, pin a tape measure to the piece just above where the line of tacks go and they'll all be perfectly spaced.

Drive in leftover tacks to a spot underneath in case any ever get lost.

Make a tool for removing upholstery tacks from a nail file. Bend an inch of the handle at a 30-degree angle and file a "V" notch in the end.

Hedge clippers make a good tool for cutting upholstery foam padding.

Or, use your electric carving knife from the kitchen.

Wicker and cane

Sagging cane seats can be firmed up by shrinking. Turn the chair upside down and wipe with water. After an hour the sag should be gone.

Better still, try this formula:

1 tablespoon of glycerin
$1/2$ gallon of warm water

Brush on the chair bottoms and watch the sag disappear.

INSTANT FURNITURE

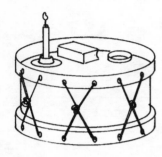

Put junk to work
An old bass drum with one head intact laid on its side will be a unique table for a den.

Four ugly, carvy turned legs from a table can become four ugly lamp bases if you'll drill for the cord to come through.

If you don't need four lamps, cut up the legs to make candle holders.

Large wooden electric cable spools can furnish your deck. Laid over on the side, the biggest size is right for a table and another size make perfect stools.

Logs from a large tree cut to the right height are sturdy stools for outdoor use.

Hold still
Lock pieces of sectional furniture together with screen door hook sets.

Bathrooms, Kitchens, and Utility Rooms

BATHROOM

Tile and Grout

Gleaming grout

The abrasiveness of a typewriter eraser will usually clean the grout between tiles. The round wheel eraser is best because it fits right into the space between the tiles.

Or, use fine sandpaper.

Automatic dishwasher liquid and an old toothbrush also does a good job.

Or, try denture cleaner and a brush. It really works!

A half cup of borax in a half gallon of water cleans and whitens grout.

Lime and scale deposits on grout and other bathroom surfaces can be removed with a tablespoon of ammonia in a quart of warm water. Soak and scrub.

Hiding the dirt

When all the cleaners fail, cover the old grout with white liquid shoe polish. It'll make yellow grout look white.

So will a nail whitener pencil. Wet it and run it along the lines.

Removing old grout

A punch-type can opener is a great tool for removing old grout between tiles.

Give this tool a handle with a section of PVC plastic pipe with a cap on one end and the other end filled with epoxy. Put the tool in before the glue sets up. Add a screw eye in the cap as a hanger.

Taking out a tile

To remove a broken tile, drill a small hole in the center.

Then use a glass cutter to score an "X" from the corners. Tap the tile and it should break along the lines. The hole is for prying the pieces out without harming surrounding tiles.

Mix and match
Matching an old tile is often impossible. Remove more and replace with a contrasting color to form a decorative pattern.

Or, use tile decals to hide the difference.

Applying new grout
If you use powdered grout and mix, make it a little thin and use a plastic squeeze bottle for shooting it in the cracks.

The rounded end of a toothbrush is a good tool for smoothing new grout.

Cleaning the tiles
Here's a homemade tile cleaner formula:

> 1 gallon warm water
> $1/2$ cup white vinegar
> 1 cup household ammonia
> $1/4$ cup baking soda

Mix well and wear your rubber gloves while using a scrub brush to clean tile to a gleaming shine.

Replacing a tile
When replacing a tile, use round toothpicks broken in half as spacers between tiles until adhesive sets up.

Or, run strips of masking tape across the face to hold.

Tubs and Showers

Caulking a tub
Before installing new tub caulk, fill the tub with water and get in. The weight will open the gap to its widest so you get plenty of caulk in place.

Use a damp finger to smooth the bead of caulk around the tub.

Tub cleaning

Fill a spray bottle with a half-water, half-bleach solution for a cleanup after each bath or shower.

Try automatic dishwasher liquid on unknown spots. Leave for an hour.

Use your regular scouring powder but dip the rag in turpentine instead of water.

Salt and turpentine also work.

Make a ring of putty to put around a stubborn spot. Then pour in some ammonia. The ring acts as a dam and holds the cleaner in place right over the spot.

For fiberglass tub and shower units, the strongest— yet safe—cleaner is the type made to clean fiberglass boats.

Rust stains

Make a paste of cream of tartar and hydrogen peroxide to remove rust stains.

Wood bleach containing oxalic acid is gangbusters on removing rust.

The flowers on the tub bottom

Remove non-slip appliques from the tub with a laundry prewash from the super market. After thirty minutes, attack with a single edge razor blade held flat against the tub. If there is adhesive left, give it a second shot.

For leftover adhesive, use a spray lubricant and a coarse rag.

Typewriter cleaning fluid also helps remove these appliques.

Leaking shower stall

The shower pan may not be leaking. The plates around where the handles come out of the wall could be the culprit. Caulk will seal these gaps.

Rather than rip out a tile shower floor to replace the shower pan, put a masonry sealer over the floor and at least one row of tiles up the wall: no water goes through the grout so the pan isn't needed.

Shower doors

Remove soap scum and water spots by brushing with warm vinegar.

Ammonia often works.

Reconstituted lemon juice does well.

Mix $^1/_4$ cup washing soda and $^1/_2$ cup each of white vinegar and ammonia into a gallon of warm water to scrub away soap scum.

After the glass doors are clean, apply a thin coat of oil furniture polish. It prevents a future buildup.

Or, spray the surface with that no-stick cooking oil spray for pans.

Clean with kerosene. It not only gets rid of soap scum, but leaves an oily film. It does have an odor but this only lasts for a day or so. 🔥

Acrylic floor treatment liquid will clean and protect the shower door.

Curtains

Machine wash shower curtains in detergent and warm water with several large bath towels. The towels do the scrubbing for you. As it goes into the rinse cycle, add a cup of vinegar. Don't spin dry; hang the curtain to dry.

Prevent water from getting out around the ends of the curtains by adding clear plastic triangles at each end. These pieces are fixed to the wall and the tub edge by silicone sealant.

The dribbling shower

Vinegar

Mineral deposits in a shower head can cut the flow of water. Remove the unit, take it apart and soak it in hot vinegar. Metal parts can be put in a pot of vinegar and brought to a boil.

If you don't want to take the head off, fill a plastic bag with hot vinegar and tie it up around the shower head.

Toilet Troubles

No sweat

A thin film of paste wax over the toilet tank may stop sweating.

Or, coat with glycerin.

Inside the tank

The running toilet (where water goes out over the top of the overflow tube) usually means the float needs to be repositioned. This can be done by *gently* bending down on the brass rod coming out of the floating ball.

Two denture cleaning tablets will clean all the parts in the tank.

A broken tank lid

If you break the toilet tank lid and can't find a match, make one of wood and paint or stain it.

By cutting holes in a wooden tank top, you have a plant holder. Short wicks hanging into the water in the tank will let the plants stay watered.

Prevent the lid from breaking by running a bead of silicone sealant around the top lip of the tank. This gives you a cushion on which to place the lid on the tank.

Bowl cleaning

Sometimes there is a line around the water level mark in the toilet. This is from mineral deposits. Use a pumice stone made for taking dead skin from elbows and feet.

Or, try sand and a wet sponge.

A fine-grit, wet/dry sandpaper will also work.

Pour in a bucket of water to flush the bowl without refilling. Then apply a paste made from borax and reconstituted lemon juice. When the paste dries, scrub with a damp brush.

Kooky as it sounds, a cola-type soft drink poured into the bowl and left overnight will do wonders.

Equally kooky. Plop a couple of denture cleaning tablets like we suggested for the tank. When the tablets are gone, so is the dirt.

Basins and Vanities

A brightener

Line the sink with paper towels soaked in laundry bleach and leave them until they dry.

A wild treatment

Any bathroom fixtures — tubs, sinks, or toilets — can be covered with fabric or wallpaper for wild decor that will also cover scratches and other things. Use epoxy glue and then cover the surface with several coats of varnish or polyurethane.

Medicine Cabinet

Shhh!

Many homes have bathrooms back-to-back and medicine cabinets back-to-back. If you'll take one cabinet out and stuff insulation between the two, you'll cut way back on noise between the two rooms.

Mirrors

A bathroom mirror is subjected to much moisture. Protect the mirror by spraying shellac over the silvered back. Test first with a cotton swab down in a corner.

Your hair dryer will remove fog from mirrors.

A thin film of glycerin will help retard the fog-up.

For a framed beveled glass mirror that needs resilvering, strip off the remaining silvering, get an inexpensive mirror cut to size, and install it behind the beveled glass.

Bathroom Accessories

Hold tight

Some soap dishes and toothbrush holders are held to tile by rubber suction cups. For better, longer-lasting adhesion, rub the suction cup across a wet bar of soap.

Instead of water, use glycerin for longevity.

Sometimes the edges of the suction cup become frayed. A sharp pair of scissors will trim away the bad edges for new holding power.

A magazine rack

Install a towel rack next to the toilet and about six inches from the floor. Magazines and books will rest on the floor and be held upright by the bar.

Make your own magazine rack for the "Library."

Privacy

Foil the peeper

Install mirror squares on the bottom sash of the bathroom window. This will keep a Peeping Tom from seeing you while the top sash still lets in light. The mirrors are great for applying makeup in natural light and may even make a tiny bath look a little larger.

Mix epsom salts and beer to an almost paste consistency. Apply this to the glass and it will dry to a frosted glass effect.

KITCHEN

Utensils

Tools of the trade
The kitchen cleaning tools—sponges, brushes, scouring pads, and the like—should be run through the dishwasher on the top rack to clean.

The Kitchen Sink

Stains on porcelain
Remove many stains from a white porcelain sink by lining it with paper towels saturated with laundry bleach. The towels cling to the sides until dry. Then rinse and rejoice!

A paste made of cream of tartar and peroxide will lift out rust spots from a porcelainized iron sink. The peroxide for hair is stronger than hydrogen peroxide.

Cream of tartar by itself on a damp rag will let you rub away many spots.

New rust stains can often be rubbed away with a lemon wedge and a little salt.

Stainless steel
Clean a stainless steel sink with automobile rubbing compound. It removes spots and leaves a thin film of wax that helps prevent future spots.

If you use other cleaners, apply oil to the surface after cleaning to prevent future spots.

Rubbing alcohol will remove many spots on stainless steel.

Or, try rubbing a lemon peel over the spots.

Shine with dry flour on a dry rag.

The stopper
A lost sink stopper can be replaced by the plastic lid from a coffee can. The weight of the water keeps it in place.

Protection against yourself
If you use the kitchen sink to wash parts, put a towel in to protect the porcelain.

Kitchen Appliances

Gleaming appliances
Mix $1/4$ cup laundry bleach and $1/4$ cup baking soda in a pint of warm water. Scrub the surface and wipe with a cloth soaked in rubbing alcohol.

After cleaning, give appliances a shine with a rub-down from wax paper.

Chipped appliances
If it's white, hide the chip with white nail polish.

Countertops

Plastic laminate stains
Stains on a plastic laminate top will usually wipe up. If not, place a folded paper towel saturated with peroxide on the stain.

Here's a freaky remedy that works on some stains. Try a solution of equal parts milk, laundry bleach, and water. Let it sit for only thirty seconds and then rinse it off. What have you got to lose?

Some stains will respond to a paste made of baking soda and water. Leave it on until the paste dries and wipe it away with a damp rag.

No shine?
Plastic laminate that's dulled from use can be shiny again with a coat of paste wax.

Chipped places
Melted crayons can be blended to match almost any color. When your color is right, fill in the boo-boos.

The big burn
A hot pan can leave its mark. If it's in an area where it would be appropriate, attach a cutting board to hide the burn.

Or, glue on a ten- or twelve-inch tile.

Cabinets and Storage

Cleaning cabinets 6
The main cause of dirty kitchen cabinets is airborne grease from cooking. Mineral spirits paint thinner on a rag will do a quick job of cleaning.

Or, try a cup of baking soda in a quart of hot water.

Pots and pans: the decorator's touch?
Paint a tree on the wall and add cut hooks at appropriate places from which you can hang pots and pans. Saves cabinet space and creates a wild mural.

Just hanging out
Pots and pans will take up less room if you use S-hooks to hang them from a chain coming down from the ceiling in a kitchen corner.

Press new space into service
The cabinet once used to house a fold-out ironing board is great for a mini pantry for small cans and spices.

Behind the door
Staple a fold-out paper file folder to the inside of a cabinet door to hold lids, trivets, and other flat kitchen items.

A recipe for keeping recipes
When you clip out recipes, keep them in a big envelope taped to the inside cover of your cookbook.

While cooking, stand a fork in a glass with the tines sticking up. Weave the recipe between tines and it's held in place where you can see it.

Hang the bags
A wooden pants hanger will clamp down on any number of paper grocery bags and can hang from a nail until a bag is needed.

Blinds for privacy
Open shelves can be covered with mini blinds that come in a variety of colors.

A shelf paper trick
Contact shelf paper will be easier to handle if stored for a while in the freezer before use.

Heat from a hair dryer will help to remove the old stuff.

Easier drawer action
Use spray wax for a quick way to lubricate the runners on a balky drawer.

The stuck drawer
The drawer with too much stuff inside can be blocked shut. Slip a spatula in at the top of the drawer and push down what's in the way.

Or, use a handsaw blade.

Reflect on this
Seldom-used high shelves hide many of their contents. Use a hand mirror to help you see what's out of sight. This also works in the shop and garage.

Stocking stuffers
If you don't have wire baskets, store potatoes and onions in an old nylon stocking hanging inside a pantry or closet.

Cutting Boards and Butcher Blocks

Stains
Remove stains from a cutting board with laundry bleach.

Or, sprinkle salt over spots and rub with a lemon wedge.

For a bigger butcher block, use half a grapefruit instead of the smaller lemon.

A paste of lemon juice and baking soda can be spread on and left overnight to lift out stains.

A new finish
After cleaning a cutting board, apply mineral oil to the top. Let it soak in and then wipe away any excess.

Or, use cooking oil.

The oil seems to penetrate better if you use a hand-held hair dryer to warm the wood before applying it.

Flatware, Cutlery, and Dishes

A knife hanger
Make cutlery holders for the inside of a cabinet door with wooden spools from the sewing room. Using glue, attach the spools in a row butted against each other. The gaps between spools receive the knife blade and the handle rests on the spools.

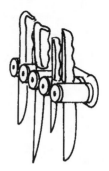

The stuck glass trick
Glasses nestled together, one inside another, tend to get stuck. Rather than risk breaking them by forcing them apart, pour cold water into the top glass and dunk the bottom one into hot water. The cold water will make the top glass contract while the hot water expands the bottom one.

Clothes pins hold plate for gluing.

Broken china
A cracked china cup can often be mended by simmering it for a half hour in milk.

Broken dishes can be glued together. To hold the dish for gluing, stick the bottom part into a container of sand with the broken edge straight up. Apply the glue and gravity will hold it in place. If you need a little extra holding help, try spring-type clothespins.

To avoid damage to china and crystal that must be hand-washed, line the sink with a towel.

Silver-lined ideas
In the absence of silver polish, toothpaste will do pretty well.

An old powder puff is great for polishing silver.

Keep a stick of chalk in with stored silverware to absorb moisture which helps to cause tarnish.

An a-peeling idea
Use the underside of a banana peel to polish and shine silver.

Small Appliances

Tea kettle whistling a sad song?
Lime deposits in your tea kettle can be cleaned out by

bringing equal parts of water and white vinegar to a boil. Then let it sit overnight. Look for lots of guck to go down the drain the next day.

Awful coffee?

If the coffee starts to taste funny, it may be time for a quick cleaning. As with the tea kettle, just brew up a half vinegar, half water solution (without the coffee grounds) and then run plain water through a brewing cycle.

Do the same thing with a baking soda and water solution.

Or, run through the cycle using Kool-Aid instead of coffee. Sounds far out but it works!

Ran out of filters?

Use part of a paper towel.

The microwave

Clean spills by placing a wet paper towel over the spot and zap it for ten to fifteen seconds. Use another towel to easily wipe up the mess.

To find out if a dish is okay for use in the microwave, place it in the unit and turn it on high for twenty seconds. If the container feels warm, don't use it.

Or, put a glass of water next to the suspect container and run on high for a minute. If the water gets hot and the dish stays cold, the dish is okay.

Blend in

Let the blender clean itself. Add a couple of drops of detergent to hot water, cover, and turn it on for a few seconds.

Oil the blender with mineral oil. There'll be no bad taste added to the food.

A shocking toast

Never poke a knife or fork into the toaster to retrieve a sliver of toast. If it's plugged in, you could get zapped.

Dull chrome

Ammonia and water will shine the chrome on small appliances.

Garbage

Bags and ties
Store a few extra trash bags and twist ties under the bag in present use. When it's full, another is standing by.

Instead of twist ties, slit an "X" in a plastic coffee can lid and poke the twisted trash bag end through this. It'll hold!

Mini trash
Hang an inexpensive plastic waste basket in the cabinet door under the sink. Drill a pair of holes near the top of the container and then hang it from cup hooks for a handy trash bin.

Wheel it out
A skateboard will make duck soup of taking out heavier, bulkier bags.

Fly trap
Glue a sticky pest strip on the underside of the garbage can lid to keep flies away.

Cleaner garbage
To clean a garbage can, use one of those rotating lawn sprinklers under the upside-down garbage can. You may have to weight the trash can down.

Rust buster
Spray auto undercoating on the bottom of a metal trash can to prevent rust.

The Laundry Room

Sock it
Keep a small quantity of liquid fabric softener in a glass jar. Leave enough room to immerse a clean sweat sock. Now, wring it out and toss the sock into the dryer along with the wet clothes from the washer. Cheap, but good.

Or, keep used softener sheets in the jar and wring one out to go into the dryer.

ATTICS

Lights

The burning string trick
Many attic and basement lights are of the pull-string variety. The string usually rests against the bulb. If left on long enough, the string can burn through. Duct tape wrapped several times around the string will insulate it against the heat.

A spare on hand
Keep an extra flashlight in the attic just in case you're up there when there's a power failure. Be sure it's easy to get to.

Winter

Cold fighters
If your home has a whole house fan, it can be causing warm air to escape into the attic. Staple a large plastic sheet over the entire unit to stay warm in the winter.

The covers over access holes should have insulation stapled over the top and some weatherstripping around the edges.

An attic door can be insulated by gluing rigid foam on it.

Entry

Something to grab
If you have to enter your attic through a scuttle hole in the closet, wouldn't it be nice to have something to use as a hand hold? Hang a rope from a rafter in a convenient place to grab.

Storage

Store a rug
Attach a pair of old belts to the rafters to hold a rolled rug for storage.

Tape a large coffee can over each end to keep pests from nesting.

The ultimate solution to a stuffed attic
If your attic is crowded, it may be time to hold a garage sale!

THE BASEMENT IS NO BARGAIN

Lighting

Free light
Improve daytime visibility by painting window wells white.

Light colors on all basement surfaces reflect more outside light.

For the blackout
Keep flashlights stashed in the basement. In case of a power failure while you're down there you might have a heck of a time finding your way up.

Or, paint the edges of the stairsteps with luminous paint.

Stairs

Painting
Rather than trapping yourself while the paint dries, just paint every other step and wait until they dry before you finish the job.

Or, paint just a third of each step, leaving a path along one side. After is dries, leave a third on the other side. The overlap will be in the center where it needs an extra coat.

Dirt

A dust stopper
Carpet the top step coming from the basement to retard tracked-in dust from the dungeon.

Storage

Posts can do double duty
A lally column, the metal post often used in basement construction, can become a round shelf unit. Cut out round shelves with a hole for the pole. Then cut them in half. Hold L-shaped brackets to the pole with worm-gear hose clamps.

Odors

It's good enough for the cows
Unfinished basement odors are hard to get rid of. Go to a farm store and get a product for sanitizing and deodorizing dairy barns. Works like a champ!

Moisture

Where's all this water coming from?
To find out, dry the area with a hair dryer and tape a piece of clear plastic over this spot. The next day, if the moisture is on the plastic it's from condensation. If under, it's coming through the floor.

The Great Outdoors

EXTERIOR PAINTING

Preparation

Cleaning up
An easy way to clean outside surfaces is to use a hose-end brush attachment made for car washing.

Mildew and yuk
Here's a magic formula for removing mildew from exterior surfaces

 3 quarts warm water
 1 quart liquid laundry bleach
 $1/4$ cup powdered detergent
 $2/3$ cup trisodium phosphate

Scrub the surfaces with a broom or brush dipped into this mix. Rinse well with water from the hose. Be sure the surfaces are dry before painting.

Scrapers

When the going gets tough
Make the paint scraper more versatile by adding a large drawer pull near the front end. Now you can work two handed!

A 2x4 with hardware cloth stapled around it is a large two-handed scraper for large flat surfaces.

Drawer knob on scraper

Protection

Plants don't like paint
Cover hedges with sheets or drop cloths.

A helping hand
One of those pant clips worn by bikers will hold the drop cloth around the bottom of shrubs and bushes.

Ladder and Scaffold Tips

Getting high
A sturdy wooden picnic table can be a good portable scaffold.

Or, use two fifty-five-gallon drums with a 2x12 walkway on top.

Look, Ma, no hands!
Use an old belt around a rung to hold a paint can.

Or, install a C-clamp around the bucket handle and the ladder rung.

Use a large plastic bucket hanging from the ladder to hold all your painting tools such as rags, scrapers, and brushes plus the paint bucket itself.

Look, Ma, no dirty hands!
Keep a container of solvent and a supply of rags near the entrance. You'll be reminded to clean up before going inside.

The Actual Painting

Another screen test
When painting window screens, the step ladder makes a nice easel. To raise the frames up off the ground, angle a wide board from the bottom step to the ground behind the ladder. The frames rest on it.

Or, attach a C-clamp to each side rail to hold the screens.

WINDOWS

Cleaning

Outside dirt is tough
Pure vinegar is a good glass cleaner for stubborn dirt.

Pure ammonia is great for removing mineral deposits where the lawn sprinkler hits the glass.

For really stubborn mineral deposits, dip a commercially soaped steel wool dish pad in ammonia and go to work.

Safety

With both feet on the ground
Clean second floor windows using a hose-end sprayer with automatic dishwashing detergent. You'll get sparkling clean glass without spots and without that death-defying ladder climb.

ROOF WORK

Patch Ups

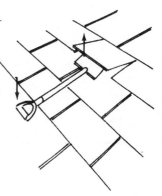

Raising the roof
To raise up a shingle to remove the one underneath, use a flat shovel and gently step on the handle.

Razing the entire roof
A flat shovel makes quick work of removing old shingles.
    Or, use a garden fork. It, too, gets underneath to lift 'em off.

Curling edges
To press down the corners of asphalt shingles, use a heat gun to make them more flexible. Then a dab of roof cement should hold them down.

Bare-headed nails
When nails have to be exposed in roof repair, put a small dab of roof cement or other sealant over the head.

Locating a leak
The best way to locate a leak is to go into the attic during a rain storm.

Flashing

Focus on flashing
Maybe you don't have to climb up to examine flashing. First try using the binoculars.

Sealer substitute
Spray automotive undercoating to patch leaks around flashing.

Roof Safety

Sneaker aid
Test your sneakers as soon as you get on the roof the be sure they have good traction.

Not all sneakers were created equal. Get extra traction by spraying the soles with auto belt dressing.

Retread your sneakers with a hot solder gun or iron. Burn crisscross lines.

Calculate from afar
To keep from having to climb up to determine the pitch of the roof, use a zig-zag rule to eyeball it and then place this against a protractor for the angle.

GUTTERS
AND DOWNSPOUTS

Cleaning

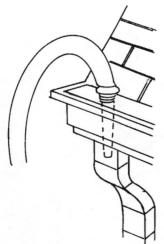

Blow it out
Put the vacuum hose in the blower opening and blow the leaves out.

Flush it out
To unclog downspouts, poke the garden hose down from the top and turn on the water.

Repairs

Fast fix
In addition to regular roofing compound, auto undercoating in aerosol form can mend gutter leaks quicker.

Gutter Painting

Quick prep
Galvanize guttering usually won't accept paint until it has

weathered for six months to a year. Instant weathering can be had by wiping all the surfaces with vinegar.

Always use a zinc-based primer on this type of gutter.

Quick finish
A dishwashing mop from the kitchen quickly slaps on the paint inside.

Downspout painting
The inside of the downspout can rust, too. But how do you get a brush inside? Drop a string with a weight down. When it comes out, replace the weight with a sponge. Force the sponge inside and then pour paint in from the top. As you pull the sponge up, it coats the insides.

PATIO AND DECK

Layout and Tryout

Get the right shape
When planning a deck or patio, outline it with a garden hose to get the shape you like.

Is it going to be big enough?
Once you've got the shape, have a pre-patio party to see if it will hold your furniture and friends. Stake it off and put your grill and furniture in place. Then invite as many people as you think you'll ever entertain outside. It's a fun way not to go wrong.

A neat way to outline before actually building is to use concrete blocks with the openings facing up. Then use the openings as pots and plant flowers in each. Very colorful. You can use this same idea for a completed patio or walk.

Or, use clay flower pots with short candles inside to outline. These are also good for lighting a walk.

Thinking ahead
Before building your deck, if it will be off the ground, plan to use the space under the deck for storage. It's easier to make cabinets while building the deck than to add them later.(Even a narrow space could be used to store a ladder.)

Pouring a Patio

Anchors

If you're going to have railings, put a small glass jar in the place where the rails will be anchored. After the patio is cured, break the glass and set the hardware with more precision.

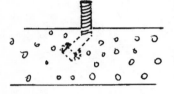

If setting anchor bolts in concrete, bend the bolt at about a forty-five-degree angle with the bend being under the surface. Be sure the exposed threads are straight up. The bolt will have much more strength.

Outdoor Furniture

Cut out the cutting

Metal tubular legs will often cut through the rubber chair tips. Not if you place a coin inside each rubber tip. And you'll always have some spare change hidden away.

Or, use a metal washer.

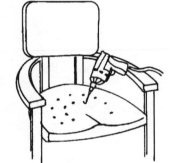

Get to the seat of the rust problem

Contoured metal chairs hold water. Drill a series of holes in an attractive design to let the water drain.

Frayed around the edges

When replacing plastic webbing, run a hot solder gun tip along the webbing ends. This melts the plastic and fuses it so it can't unravel.

Bugs

A win/win situation

Buy your nearest neighbor an electronic bug zapper. He'll think you're super. His bug zapper light will also lure most of the bugs away from your yard.

Cookouts

Keep the charcoal dry

Use a small plastic trash can with the lid painted black to store briquettes and keep them dry.

Cleaning the grill
Oven cleaner will do a great job outdoors, too.

Quicker cleanup
After cooking on a gas grill turn the gas off, and while the grill is still hot, cover it with wet newspaper. By the time you're finished eating, you can just wipe the grill clean.

Meals on wheels
Use an old metal-bed wheelbarrow with a grate across the top and you have a grill that can roll to the pool, patio, or lawn.

Instant grill
Make a quick grill from concrete blocks stacked in a U-shape with an oven shelf laid on top as a grill. For the base, use either a concrete stepping stone or the ground.

POOL PLAY

Slippery Steps

A step in the right direction
If you ever have to drain your pool, take that occasion to stick down some of those bathtub appliques so swimmers always have good footing when entering the pool.

Shower

Make your own
Make an outdoor shower from PVC pipe. Attach it to the fence by the pool and use a garden hose for water supply.

FENCE ME IN

Posts

On the level
A garden hose can serve as your super long level when there is a slope in the yard. Tape one end of the hose to the highest post. Pour water into the hose. When the water starts to come out the other end, have a helper

raise the hose until water quits running out and stays level with the end. That point is level with the top of the first post and lets you set the next post.

Mixed up about concrete?
Give a squirt of liquid detergent into the mix along with the water. This yields a creamier mixture that's easier to work with.

No mixing
Just pour the pre-mixed dry ingredients into the hole around the post. Then take a stick and, as you pour small quantities of water in, poke the mix. (If the ground is very dry, dampen the hole before you pour in the dry mix.)

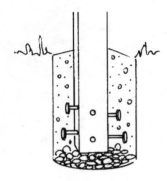

A stronger anchor
When setting metal posts in concrete, drill holes in the post part that will be underground. This way, mix will ooze into the holes, making the post more securely anchored.

Drive large nails part way into the bottom of a wooden post so the concrete has something extra to hold onto.

Or, staple chicken wire to the lower part of the post for better holding power when the concrete is poured.

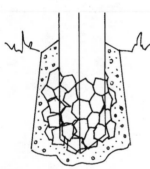

Keep the water out
Put a bead of caulk around the seam where the post meets the concrete. No water can seep in to rot or rust.

Or, pull a plastic bag up around the bottom of the post. After the concrete sets up, trim away the excess and seal the edge with silicone sealant.

Chicken wire anchors post to concrete.

Post set in con-crete.

Plastic posts
Large-sized plastic drain pipe can be used as fence posts. After setting the post in concrete, insert a couple of lengths of reinforcing steel in the upright pipe and then pour concrete into the pipe. Use a plastic cap over the top.

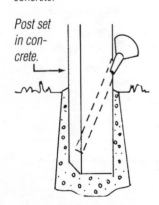

Preserving the wood
A post that's already set in concrete can still be treated against rot. Drill holes at an angle down into the post, taking care not to go all the way through. Pour a preservative and then cap the holes with dowels. Repeat annually.

Slanted hole lets you funnel preservative to post below surface.

A rotten idea

If you have a post rotting underground, prop it with a
metal post made for wire fences. Get the kind that's flat
on one side and drive it into the ground against the wood
post. When the metal post is screwed to the wood post,
your fence will again be sturdy.

Sagging and dragging

A too-large gate may start to sag. Install a furniture caster
in the end and the gate rolls along.

Fence Improvements

Stay open!

A couple of magnetic cabinet door catches will hold the
gate open.

No prying eyes

For privacy, shingle a picket fence. Looks good, too.

Fence Painting

The cheap coat

Whitewashing was made popular as a fence coating by
Tom Sawyer. There are still those who use this cheap
cover-up. Here are a couple of my favorite formulas.
However, with each you need to first make lime paste by
mixing fifty pounds of hydrated lime to six gallons of
water. This yields the eight gallons of lime paste called
for. Here goes:

> 15 pounds salt
> 5 gallons water
> 8 gallons lime paste

Dissolve salt in water and then stir in lime paste.
Should be the consistency of whole milk. If not, thin with
more water.
Or, try the

Super Handyman's Trial and Error Special

> 6 pounds salt
> 3 gallons water
> 8 gallons lime paste
> 3 pounds white Portland cement
> 3 tablespoons laundry bluing

Dissolve salt in boiling water. When cool, blend in lime and then cement. Add bluing as you go. If too thick to mix, add water. When complete, thin to milk consistency.

Whitewash rolls on best over a dampened surface.

Mix it in a wheelbarrow and roll it along as needed.

Avoid overspray

When painting a chain link fence, use a sprayer but have someone on the other side with a large appliance carton to catch the overspray before it gets on the neighbor's Rolls Royce.

MASONRY

Concrete

Tired of tamping?

Many times concrete is poured over a bed of tamped sand. The spare tire from the car is a great tamper.

Or, use a large fireplace log.

Make a tamper from a 4x4 post with screen door handles on each side.

Leftover mix?

It's a good idea to have small alternate projects in case there's any leftover concrete.

Stepping stones are a good alternate. Use a garbage can lid as a form for round stones. Coat it with oil for easier release.

Make a hardboard divider to fit down into a coffee can. Pour the leftover concrete into the can and, when it sets up, you'll have a pair of concrete book ends. Glue felt on the bottoms to protect the shelf surface.

Or, how about a boat anchor? Pour mix into a coffee can and insert a large eyebolt before it sets up.

Leftover dry cement

Never store bags of cement directly on a concrete floor. It may absorb moisture and turn into a big rock.

Make a wooden platform to hold sacks up.

Or, use an old auto tire as your platform.

Store the bag in a bag—a sealed plastic trash bag, that is.

This cracks me up

Small cracks can be filled with auto body filler.

For filling hairline cracks, try wearing a rubber glove and just dipping a finger into the mix and rubbing it into the crack.

Easier lifting

Slide a bag of concrete onto a snow shovel and slide it rather than straining your back.

Criss-cross a pair of belts around a bag of cement for easier lifting.

Make your own concrete paint

Mix white Portland cement into skim milk until it reaches a paint consistency and you'll have an excellent concrete paint.

Brick Work

Making mortar joints match

To age new mortar joints, pat them with a wet tea bag until they match the old.

Lighten mortar by adding white chalk dust.

Darken by adding lampblack.

Add color to mortar by mixing in colored chalk dust.

In small places where mortar is missing, fill with silicone sealant and then blow ground up mortar dust into the wet sealant. Enough will stick to make it look like the real thing.

Handling the raking

The end of a toothbrush handle can be a good tool for raking mortar joints.

Removing a brick

When you must remove a brick, use a masonry bit to drill out as much mortar as possible before using a chisel for the rest. Use a pair of marbles per brick to act as spacers.

A hang up

If you need to hang something from a brick wall, drilling in the mortar joints is easier and often better than drilling in the brick.

Quick retaining wall

Stack bags of ready-mixed concrete to form the wall. Drive steel rebar down through the bags. Wet completely and, when the bags set up, you have a sturdy wall.

Walks

Your own design

Make a unique design on a freshly poured walk by pressing the open end of a tin can into the mix.

Or, embed rock salt. After the concrete cures, water will dissolve the salt and leave an interesting pockmarked surface.

The memory walk

Who hasn't put their name or initials in some newly poured concrete? Enjoy making a walk that is a family history. Put hand prints of all the family along with their names. Make note of all the birth dates and any other important day in history. Like when you broke 100 on the golf course.

Stepping stone walks

In laying out a stone walk across a lawn, just place the stones down atop the grass. When it looks right, sprinkle flour over the walk. When the stones are removed, you have an outline of exactly where to dig.

When pouring stepping stones, you can use coat hanger wires for reinforcement.

Or, cut out pieces of chicken wire.

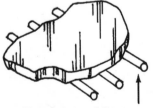

Pipes help to roll flat stone.

Rolling stones

Instead of lifting heavy chunks, use a pry bar to raise the edge and roll a pipe under the stone. Lift the other edge and slip in a second pipe. Now the stone will roll and, as you move a few inches, slip in a third pipe. As a pipe rolls out the back, place it under the front of the stone.

Driveways

Grease and oil spots

Oil spots are the bane of driveways. Saturate the spot with paint thinner and then cover with an absorbent such as cat litter, sand, sawdust, dry Portland cement, cornmeal, or the like. Wait overnight and sweep away the absorbent and the spots.

Rusty looks
Rust spots respond to wood bleach products that contain oxalic acid.

Or, make a past of ammonia and baking soda. Scrub this into the spot and hose it away after an hour or so.

A tip-top blacktop tip
Scatter marble chips meant for landscaping over blacktop drives for better looks and to reflect some of the summer heat from the sun.

Keep off the grass!
Brush on luminous paint along the edges of your circular driveway to help keep cars from ruining the lawn.

FIREWOOD

Cutting Remarks

Protection for the chainsaw
Cut the leg from an old pair of blue jeans and sew up one end. You now have a sleeve for the chain and bar.

Retire unsteadiness
Make a rig to hold logs upright for splitting by nailing a foot-long section of an old tire to a 2x6 scrap.

Or, stack a couple of tires and the log will stand in the ring.

A Cord of Wood

Is it all there?
Firewood is usually sold by the cord. How much is a cord? The magic number is 128 cubic feet. The stack should be four feet wide by four feet high by eight feet long or the equivalent. Since most fireplaces won't take a log that's four feet long, you're more likely to be looking at two feet wide by four feet high by sixteen feet long.

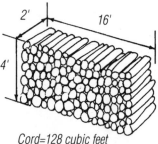

Cord=128 cubic feet

Wood Storage

A bug house?

Don't make your wood pile right on the ground. It attracts too many bugs. Build a frame of scrap 2x4s on concrete blocks. This allows plenty of air to circulate so the logs are kept dry, too.

Keeping dry

Stack firewood with the bark facing up. Bark repels water so you start with dryer logs.

So you'll always have a supply of dry wood, keep a supply in a large plastic garbage can at the back door.

An old dog house up at the back door also protects the logs and looks good, too.

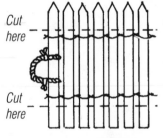

Cut here

Cut here

Tote that log!

Make a log tote from a section of old picket fence. Cut off the top and bottom just outside of the twisted wires. Add a rope handle.

A child's little red wagon is the ideal conveyance for hauling logs from the pile to the house.

If there's snow on the ground, the child's sled takes over.

THE GARAGE

Organizing

Parking right

Paint stripes using a luminous paint on the end wall of the garage to let you aim your car in and to leave adequate room on each side.

When to stop

If you're the type that has to hit the end of the garage to know that you're far enough in, why not attach an old tire at bumper level to save the car and the end of the garage.

A sponge rubber ball hanging from a string so it just barely touches the windshield in the center of the driver's face will let you know when to stop.

Attach a landscape timber to the garage floor so that the front tires will touch it just before the bumper touches the end wall.

Follow the white lines

Stripe the garage floor with white lines to indicate where big items such as bikes or mowers can stay without being in the way of the cars.

Protect the car door

Position a section of old inner tube on the garage wall so when you open the car door it doesn't get damaged if it hits the wall.

Or, use carpet scraps, foam rubber upholstery padding, or rigid foam insulation pieces for the same protection.

Lighting

Just whistle or clap

Plug in a sound activated light so you'll never be in the dark when in the garage.

Garage Storage

Your own space program

For extra storage in the garage, suspend a cabinet from the garage ceiling to utilize the unused space above the hood.

A bag of goodies

Hang a shoe bag inside a garage closet door or on the wall to hold dozens of small items.

The keeper of the keys

Attach the spine from a three-ring looseleaf notebook horizontally on the garage wall. You'll have three hooks for extra keys.

Cleaner Floors

Oil and grease spots 6

Saturate oil or grease spots with paint thinner. While it's still wet, cover the area with an absorbent. Cat litter works fine, as does sand, dry cement, baking soda, sawdust, or cornmeal. Several layers of newspaper will act as an absorbent. Leave it overnight and when you sweep it up, the spots are gone.

Or, make a paste of liquid bleach and powdered detergent. Cover the spots generously and don't remove until completely dry.

Or, make a past of liquid bleach and powdered detergent. Cover the spots generously and don't remove until completely dry.

Another way to use liquid bleach is to saturate paper towels with it and then lay several layers over the spots. When the towels are dried out, lift and if the spot isn't gone, pour on some more.

Or, saturate with engine degreaser and use fireplace ashes as an absorbent.

Make your own floor sweep

This formula is an ideal sweeping compound for the garage floor:

> 4 cups of sawdust
> 1 cup of mineral oil

Slowly add the oil to the sawdust, stirring as you go. Keep in a closed container.

Or, mix equal parts of sawdust and dried, used coffee grounds. Add enough oil to just coat all the dry stuff.

Doors and Openers

Don't open blindly

Never hit the automatic opener transmitter until you can actually see the door. It could cause an accident if another family member had opened the door and was either walking or driving under it.

You'll get a buzz out of this

Wire a buzzer so that it goes off when the garage door is opened. That way you'll know if there is an accidental opening from a stray signal.

Door springs

If your door has a spring on each side and you need to stretch them and aren't strong enough to pull them far enough, do it a little at time. Put metal washers or coins between the coils. When stretched to the proper length, hook the spring and remove the spacers.

THE GARAGE SALE

Advertising

The movable yard sign
If you can't put up signs, use the washable white paint kids use to paint slogans on the car before the big game. Just paint "Garage Sale" and park in the front drive.

Transit advertising
Signs on the kids and their bikes can reach a lot of people to and from and even in the mall.

A quick but sturdy yard sign
If you can put up signs, here's a neat trick. Use a hole in a big concrete block. Put the sign in the hole and then wedge it in place. It won't blow over.

Gardening

YARD WORK

Lawn Care

Mowing
Vary your mowing pattern each week to prevent mower tire tracks.

Put zing in your fertilizing
When fertilizing a lawn, if the spreader skips spots, your lawn will have zebra-like streaks.

Add flour to the spreader along with the fertilizer and you'll see where the stuff is being distributed and avoid the skips.

Flowers

The seed bagger
To collect seeds from annuals, put a plastic bag over the plant before digging it up. Shake vigorously and the bag catches the seeds.

Outsmart the seedlings
Before planting seedlings in a tin can, drill a hole in the bottom and drop a lid into the can. When it's time for transplanting, use a pencil to push lid, plant, and soil out.

The mobile hot bed
Keep seedlings in a child's little red wagon with a plastic sheet over it. If there's a sudden cold snap, roll it inside. When it's time to transplant, roll it out to the beds.

PVC pipe plus polyethylene for greenhouse

The mini hot house

Before the weather warms up, protect seedlings under the top half of a plastic jug with the cap off.

The movable greenhouse

Use PVC plastic pipe with three right-angle fittings at each end plus a clear plastic vapor barrier to make a mini-greenhouse. Look at the drawing and you'll see how easy the design is.

Wooden planter boxes

To preserve the inside of a wooden planter box without endangering the plants, paint with tree paint.

 Or, char the insides with a propane torch.

Weeds

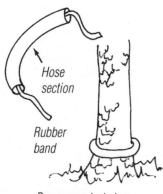

Sharpened notch in hoe cuts weeds.

A weed whacker

File a "V" notch in the side of your hoe for snipping off that occasional weed in the lawn.

Weeds in concrete

To remove weeds that grow up through cracks in concrete and other odd places, pour a salt and water solution into the crack. The weeds are gone forever.

 Ice cream salt works even better.

Poison ivy pointers

Clean your tools after cutting poison ivy, as you can still be affected by the oils on the tool.

 Never burn poison ivy, as the smoke can carry particles.

Trees and Shrubs

Hose section

Rubber band

Bumper protects tree from mower.

A bumper crop

Protect your trees from damage from the mower by installing a bumper around the trunk. A section of garden hose with a length of rubber band cut from an inner tube will take the bumping. The rubber band expands as the tree grows.

You'll dig this
When planting large items such as trees and shrubs, you can at least make refilling the hole a little easier. Spread a large trash bag or other sturdy plastic sheet out and pile the dirt on it as you dig. When the plant is in place, lift the edges of the plastic up and the dirt will slide back in.

A back saver
For easier moving of a big plant, slide it on to a flat shovel and drag it along.

Hedge trimming
Place a plastic drop cloth under hedges and shrubs so all the clippings will fall on it for a super easy pick-up.

Circling around
In landscaping around a tree, you can dig a perfect circle by looping a rope around the tree and putting the shovel inside the loop. Pull it tight and the shovel can move only that fixed distance away from the trunk.

Trees at stake
Old lamp cord is good when staking a tree as it won't cut through the bark.

Potato appeal
Before planting a new tree, line the hole with baking potatoes. They help hold moisture and, as they decay, nutrients are released.

A pruning point
For high pruning, add an extension handle to a bow saw made from lightweight conduit pipe.

Stumped on getting rid of a tree stump?
Drill as many holes as deep as you can and then pour water over the stump. Cover it with dirt or plastic and let Mother Nature do the work.

For faster decay of a stump, pour buttermilk into holes drilled into the stump. Bacterial action sets in.

Or, convert it into a planter. Nail a metal band around the top of the stump, fill this with soil, and plant in it.

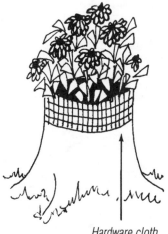

Hardware cloth

Birds roosting

Flocks of birds pick out a single tree as their roosting place. To drive them away, get twenty or thirty tennis balls in several colors. Stand and toss the balls into the tree. The birds will leave . . . but they'll soon come back. Do it again. Pretty soon they'll pick out another tree . . . or your arm will fall off.

Leaves

It's in the bag

Bring a trash bag through a sleeve made by removing top and bottom from a corrugated box. Hold the bag in place with clothes pins. The device lies flat on the ground for easy raking into the bag.

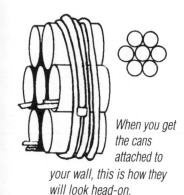

When you get the cans attached to your wall, this is how they will look head-on.

Garden Hoses and Watering

Hose storage

It's best to store your hoses rolled up. A wheel from a car can be mounted to a wall or post as a good hose holder.

Make your own hose holder for in the garage with seven two-pound coffee cans, screwed to the wall with large screws. Center one can and form a circle around it with the others, with the open ends facing out. The hose goes around the outside and the open cans become bins for nozzles, gloves, and other small items.

Or, use two coffee cans attached to adjacent wall studs and then coil the hose in a figure eight.

An old car tire can hold the coil of hose and will roll to where you need to use the hose.

Pair of coffee cans as hose rack

Slice four six-inch sections from an old tire. Mount these U-shaped pieces in a pattern as shown with the open ends aimed away from the center. This will hold a coiled hose.

A bushel basket holds a coil of hose and is easy to carry.

Coil a small hose around a wooden coat hanger and hang it from the wall.

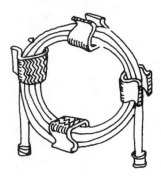

Enough water?

It's not easy to tell when the sprinkler has been on long enough. Use a rain gauge and time to see when the sprinkler brings the gauge up to the right place. From then on, you know how long to let it run.

Tired of holding the hose?

Use a "D" handled fork stuck into the ground to do the holding. Just poke the hose through the opening and then bring it over the top and back through again. It'll stay in place as long as you wish.

Or, poke a wire coat hanger into the ground and bend it to hold the hose.

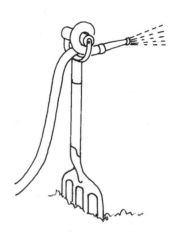

A lucky break

They say if you find a horseshoe it brings good luck. If you find a pair, it's lucky for your garden hose. Nail them to adjacent studs with the open ends up. The coiled hose hangs in there.

Garden hose hangs from lucky horseshoes.

A flower bed watering system

For an underground watering system along the entire length of a flower bed, bury a PVC plastic pipe with holes drilled along the entire length. At each end, use an elbow to bring a short pipe above the surface. To water, poke a hose into the exposed pipes and water will come out all the way along the bed.

Nozzle control

No more lost hose nozzles! A broom clip mounted to the side of the house next to the hydrant will act as a convenient holder for the nozzle.

Or, drive a nail only part way in. Slide the nozzle over it.

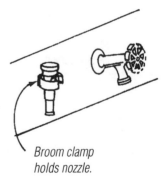

Broom clamp holds nozzle.

A heady idea

If you have underground sprinklers, edging around the sprinkler heads becomes easy with a homemade edger. Find a tin can the right diameter and sharpen the rim with your grinder wheel. Next punch a couple of holes on the side near the bottom. Rig a string through these holes and you can place the edger over the head and press down with your foot while holding the can firmly against your shoe with the strings.

Protect the hose

When trying to pull the hose around the corner of the house, the sharp edge can damage the hose. Also, the

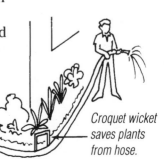

Croquet wicket saves plants from hose.

Clamp-on pants hanger closes soaker hose at desired length.

hose can damage your prize plants in a flower bed. Install a wire croquet wicket at the corner of the bed and it keeps the hose away from the plants and the house.

A large stake will do the same job but might look better if it's painted green.

Or, drive a metal stake into the ground and drop a four-to-six-inch scrap of PVC pipe over the stake.

A short soak

If you have a small area that requires a soaker hose but don't have a short soaker, temporarily shorten it with a wooden clamp-on pants hanger.

For little squirts

For a small leak in a plastic hose, just barely touch that spot with a hot solder gun tip.

If there are too many holes to patch, use an ice pick and turn it into a soaker hose.

Gentler trickler

When you leave the hose in a flower bed to trickle water in, eventually the flow will form a small gully. Attach either a sweat sock or a cotton glove with a rubber band over the end of the hose and the water is well dispersed.

Hosiery plus hose equals gentle flow.

Gardening Goodies

Sit a spell

If you're a lazy gardener and would like to work while sitting, a child's wagon will let you do it.

Or, sit facing backwards on a small trike.

A thorny problem

Some people plant thorny bushes under windows as a burglar deterrent. The crook gets cut up before he can get to the window to break in. But what happens when you need to trim 'em? Use barbecue tongs to hold thorny branches out of your way.

Spooking away garden pests

If birds are eating your seeds of vegetables, you need a scarecrow. A child's pinwheel toy will move with the least little breeze and will scare birds away.

Or, run strings across the area and let strips of

aluminum foil hang from them. The shiny, moving strips spook birds.

Even better, tie tin can lids from the strings in pairs so they hit against each other when they move. You've got noise and motion.

A dog and cat repellent
Here's a magic formula to keep dogs and cats from using flower beds and gardens:

> 1 part cayenne pepper powder
> 1 1/2 parts dry mustard powder
> 2 1/2 parts flour

Put the ingredients in a grocery bag, grasp the top and shake to mix. Then spread it where you want the animals to steer clear.

Nothing depressing about this
A storebought cat repellent can be sprayed on the top part of medical tongue depressors. Stick the bottom part into the ground where you don't want the cats to play.

More repelling thoughts
Wild animals often strip bark off trees and eat plants and crops. If you live near the zoo, get them to give you a load of lion droppings. I'm told this scares away any and all animals from the area. After the animals have learned to stay away, work the stuff into the soil and have roaring plants.

Spreading moth crystals around the edge of your garden will keep small animals from harvesting your crops.

Making tracks
When planting seeds, you can lay out the rows in a straight line by using a child's wagon with enough weight to leave tracks as you roll it across the garden. It makes two rows with each pass.

Laying out the garden
When unwinding a ball of twine, it can sort of run away from you. To keep the twine in line, poke a trowel into the ground and slip the ball over the handle.

Trowel holds ball of string

Sponge in strip from inner tube equals knee pads.

Please your knees

For groveling in the garden, make knee pads from a sleeve cut from an old innertube. Cut out a place for the back of the knees. Put a sponge in for padding.

Or, put an old pillow in a plastic trash bag. It's waterproof and comfy for kneeling.

Or, an old hot water bottle can be stuffed with rags.

Insects and Pests

It's Miller time!

Snails and slugs like beer. Pour some in a shallow pan and the next day you'll have some snails and slugs that died with smiles on their faces.

Get nasty

Nasturtiums are said to repel aphids, so plant them among other plants the bugs attack.

Onion rings

Intermingle onion and garlic plants with other flower and vegetables. Or, plant a ring of these pungent plants around others. They repel many insects.

Straw vote

Slit sections of soda straws put around the main stem of plants being attacked by cut worms will give them protection.

Mulching

Hot off the presses

Newspapers can be used as mulch. Spread them out and poke holes where you want to plant. Cover them with a layer of dirt. They retard weeds, hold the soil in place, and conserve water. They are also biodegradable.

Flip your lids

A layer of a couple of inches of bottle caps (without plastic liners) covered with dirt is a good mulch. They also rust and become iron for plants while doing the mulchy things.

Screen out the weeds

Put scraps of metal window screen under trees as mulch.
Water goes in but weeds won't grow through. As the
screen rusts, it gives some nutrients to the tree.

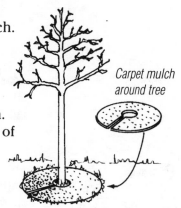

*Carpet mulch
around tree*

The red carpet treatment

An old carpet (any color will do), can be used as mulch.
Around a tree, you might wish to cut a circle or square of
carpet with a hole in the center a little larger than the
trunk. Make a slit from this hole to the edge. Put this
around the tree and cover with a half inch of dirt.

A Heap about Composting

From one heap to another

Poke holes in the sides of an old garbage can to house
your compost heap.

Better composting

Drill holes, top to bottom, in a section of plastic plumbing
pipe and poke it down all the way through the compost
pile. Water will go all the way through the heap.

Composting in a bag

Use a plastic trash bag filled with leaves, twigs, grass
clippings, vegetable peels, or other biodegradable matter.
Add a shovel of dirt. Then pour in a mix of four cups of
high nitrogen fertilizer in two gallons of water. Seal the
bag with a twist tie. Turn it a couple of times a week,
being careful not to break the bag. You'll soon have
compost.

Grass Fires

Mop up this problem

If this problem starts beyond the reach of hoses, a bucket
of water and a mop will let you beat the fire out.

YARD TOOLS

Mowers

A slick trick
Brush used motor oil under the housing of the mower to help keep grass clippings from collecting under there.
Oven cleaner will help clean the housing.

Housing insurance
Automobile undercoating spray will prevent rust from attacking the underside of the housing.

The sharper image
When hand sharpening the mower blade, use a step ladder and C-clamp as shown to anchor the blade. Flip the blade to file the other end.

Stop the shakes
Vibration is usually from an unbalanced blade. Stick a pencil or screwdriver blade through the center hole and the part of the blade that swings down is the side that needs more filing.

Added handle

An uplifting experience
A screen door handle mounted on the front of the housing of a rotary mower will make it easier to lift.

It's a gas!
At the beginning of mowing season, don't use gas left over from last year. It can gum up the works.

Mothballing the mower
Before storing for the season, remove the spark plug and put a tablespoon of motor oil into this hole. Turn the mower over a couple of time to distribute the oil.

Fireworks outlawed
If you use an electric mower, before you mow over the electric cord, wrap it with colorful tape in a spiral pattern to make it more visible. Otherwise, you may have some fireworks that rival the 4th of July.

Don't retire an old mower
Strip away the motor of the mower to be discarded and

you have a flat surface with wheels and a handle for moving heavy plants and such.

Rakes and Hoes

Better grip
Slip a section of old auto radiator hose over rake or hoe handles for a better—as well as kinder and gentler—grip. Tape the grips in place.

Stand up straight
Put a crutch tip on the ends of rake and hoe handles so the tool can lean against a wall without slipping.

Digging Tools

Pedal power
For greater digging power weld a six-inch strip of angle iron to a fork or shovel at the place where your foot goes.

Deep enough?
You'll never dig deeper than you have to if you'll mark the inches from the end on up the handle. This works on hand trowels, too.

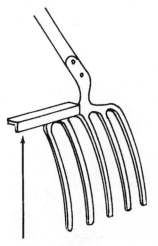

Extra foot-power

What the devil is a dibble?
If you were to cut off the handle of a garden fork or a shovel with a "D" handle and sharpen the point, you'd have a dibble, a digging tool to plant bulbs or seeds. So, if you have a broken tool handle, you know what to do with it.

Foot joy
For greater foot comfort, slip a section of slit garden hose over the part of a digging tool where your foot goes.

Identifying Your Tools

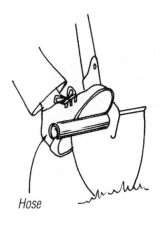

Hose

Branding time
Put your initials on all wooden tool handles by printing them with clear fingernail polish. Before it dries, set a match to it and it'll burn 'em just like a branding iron.

Color me mine
Use leftover bright paint over all parts of yards tools. It makes the tool hard to overlook in the yard. Also it's hard for your neighbor to see a bright orange tool and not remember he borrowed it from you.

Foiling the Tool Thief

Too old to be good
Nobody borrows or steals old, beat up tools. Rub dirt and grime into the handles of new tools and wrap some tape around the handle. They'll look too beat up to interest anyone. Friction tape around the garden hose will make it look bad.

Storage

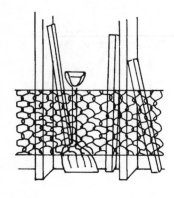

Stowing stunts
Before storing yard tools, coat the handles with linseed oil and after a few minutes, wipe away the excess. The tool will be protected during the off-season and next spring the wood will be kinder to your hands.

Staple strips of chicken wire across exposed studs and you'll have bins in which to store long-handled yards tools. (This trick also works for storing long boards and pipe in the shop.)

Cart the tools
A retired golf bag and pull cart can haul lots of yard tools around. The pockets will take care of small tools and gloves. It's also a good place to store them when not in use.

Cleaning Tools

Lube and clean
Keep a bucket of sand soaked with used motor oil handy for cleaning dirt from digging tools. Just poke the tool in and out a few times. The sharp sand cleans and the oil will stay on for protection.

Wheelbarrows

Stand-up storage
The wheelbarrow can be held in place against the wall with a screen-door spring hooked across the handles.

Three-wheel drive
Put small casters on the legs and when you need to hop curbs, these rear wheels let you raise the front wheel and go forward until you're over the top.

Casters on wheelbarrow legs aid in climbing over curb.

Tilt-proof
Install bicycle training wheels to the sides to act as outriggers and prevent wheelbarrow tipover.

Room at the top
Raise the height of your wheelbarrow with a lightweight frame covered with chicken wire. It'll just about double the capacity of leaves it can carry.

HOUSEPLANTS

Lighting

Let there be light
Plants love light so keep windows clean for more of it.

A plant that loves light needs to be rotated or it will become lopsided from reaching out toward the light.

Give your newly potted plants a little less light for several days.

A hanging basket can be suspended from a swivel from your fishing tackle box for easy turning to face the light.

Moving

For the heavy plants
Some houseplants are too heavy to lift. Slip a scrap of carpet under the pot and pull the pot along behind you.

Repaint a child's wagon to fit the decor. Put that big plant on it for easier hauling in and out.

Watering

The drinking habit
If the hanging basket doesn't have a saucer, slip a shower cap over the bottom at watering time.

Or, hang an open umbrella upside down under the plant until the dripping stops.

When plants are dying out too fast, cover pot and plant with clear plastic to keep it moist longer. This also takes care of watering when you'll be gone a few days.

Place a bottle cap over the hole in the bottom of a flower pot and excess water can seep out but the dirt won't desert your plant.

Or, use a circle cut from a scrap of plastic window screen.

A small wad of nylon net or even steel wool will do the same thing.

Or, use a small square of sponge.

Leftover tea can be used to water indoor plants. Ferns really love a spot of tea.

A stale bottle of club soda is also a popular drink for plants.

Pasta water from cooking spaghetti is also great. Cool it first.

If it's time to clean the fish tank, use the old water to make houseplants smile.

Drainage

Better run-off
Many green-thumbers swear by a layer of charcoal in the bottom of each pot.

From the peanut gallery
A layer of plastic packing pieces, often peanut shaped, can provide good drainage in the bottom of a pot.

Cleaning

A clean plant is a happy plant
A feather duster will do a great job of dusting the leaves of houseplants.

Potting Soil

Make your own
Maybe you'd like to make your own potting soil and thereby save some serious money. Fill a baking pan with about four inches of dirt from the backyard. Cover and seal with aluminum foil and insert a meat thermometer into the center of the dirt. Turn on the oven and heat to 200 degrees. Don't let it get above 200 degrees. Cook for thirty minutes and let cool over night. It's great weed-free, germ-free soil but the cooking throws off an unpleasant odor . . . big time!

Hair today, grown tomorrow
Hair has many nutrients that are beneficial to plants. Ask your hair stylist for a sack of hair and work it into the potting soil.

Houseplant Health

Medicare blossoms
When reusing a pot, give it a bath in five parts water to one part bleach. Let it soak overnight and then rinse it well. It'll be free of bugs and disease.

A dose of castor oil makes most plants hardier, healthier, and greener.

Mix equal parts of milk and water to give the plant more shiny leaves.

Tooling Around

Dig this
An old metal shoe spoon makes a dandy digger for potted plants.

After using a tool around a sick plant, clean it with liquid laundry bleach so it can't pass along insects or disease.

All in the Family: Kids, Pets, Recreation

KIDS

Kid Pleasers

Sand castles
A large truck tire can be placed flat on the ground and filled with sand for a great sandbox.

Chalk this up
Chalkboard paint lets you convert any door or wall into a chalkboard.

Special wallpaper
Paper a child's room with posters or road map that will be more interesting than a floral pattern . . . and that will cost practically nothing.

Help For Parents

The toy box trick
A plastic laundry basket is a good toy box that lets the kid see what's inside without having to pull everything out.

Feeding time at the zoo
Put a paint drop cloth under the high chair at feeding time.

    Install a towel bar on the back of the highchair to hold a towel or a wet rag for quick cleanups.

I spy
Replace your child's regular door with a weatherstripped, glass storm door. This lets you see in without making any noise.

    Or, install a security viewer in the regular door.

High jumping

If Junior uses the bed as a trampoline, chances are the slats will come loose. Install L-shaped brackets to hold the slats to the frames.

Or, run a wire with a turnbuckle in the center to pull both sides of the frame in tight.

The budding artist

Paint thinner will remove crayon marks from walls.

Or, use a spray lubricant.

To prevent marks on the wall, tape a strip of brown wrapping paper all along the wall and let the kids paint all the murals they wish.

A day at the beach

When you're ready to leave the beach, toss all the toys in a mesh bag and dip them in the ocean to clean all the sand off.

NOT SO STUPID
PET TRICKS

Dog Days

Feeding time

An old auto floor mat is great under Rover's dish. No scooting and easier cleanup.

If you use canned dog food, open both ends of the can for easier removal. You just push the food out.

Store dry dog food in a plastic garbage can. It's neater and, besides, rodents chew through the paper bags.

Slip him a pill

If you're having a problem getting a pill down your pet's throat, wrap it in a blob of ground meat or canned dog food.

A vacuum bath

If it's not traumatic to your pet, the vacuum cleaner hose attachment is a great way to avoid a messy bath.

No burrs here

For long-haired dogs with burrs caught in the hair, use

pliers to crush the burr and they'll be easier to remove.

Or, try soaking them with cooking oil; the burrs come out much more easily.

Corny dog
Cornmeal can be rubbed into pet fur to clean it. Rub it in and brush it out. Repeat this using baking soda and deodorize.

Bath time
Add baking soda to the rinse water after a tub bath for a better smelling dog.

Or, pour in some lemon juice.

Cut holes for your arms and head in an old shower curtain and hang it up. When bathing your dog, you'll still get wet but the floor won't.

A non-slip rubber or vinyl mat in the tub will make a nervous pet feel more secure.

Put one of those nylon kitchen scrubbers over the bathtub drain and pet hair will be caught instead of going down to clog up the drain.

Or, turn a tea strainer upside down and place it over the drain.

The new puppy
A new puppy won't be as likely to whine the first few nights if you wrap a hot water bottle in a soft blanket. He'll snuggle up to it just like it was his mom.

The ticking of a big alarm clock also helps keep him quit.

Put a t-shirt or some piece of clothing that you just took off next to him. Your scent will help him not to feel deserted.

If you leave during the daytime, turn the radio on so your pet won't feel so alone. No heavy rock music, though. He could turn into a hippy. Use this for your grown dog, too.

That outgrown playpen from the attic can be a new pet's corral. Staple chicken wire around the bottom so Bowser can't escape.

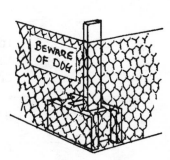

It's easy to set up a temporary fence for an outside pup by wedging 2x4 scraps into cinder block openings and then stapling chicken wire to form the pen.

The water dish
An angel food cake pan with a stake through the center hole is a pet water disk that can't be knocked over.

Stay off the couch
If you don't want Prince to sit on your imported sofa, put a whoopie cushion under the sofa cushions. When the pet gets up there, the noise will send him packing. After a few times, he'll be cured.

Or, spread a few mothballs under the cushions.

The surprise on the rug
Place a slice of raw onion over the spot where your pet made a mistake. After a day or so, he'll be discouraged from using that same place. (Now you know why so many dogs are named Spot.)

Or, spray on some cologne or perfume.

Chewing up his dog house?
Make a paste of alum and water to spread over the places being chewed. This will break him of the habit.

Or, brush oil of clove on. This can even be put on furniture legs to stop this bad habit.

Pet hair
Remove pet hair from upholstery by rubbing with a barely damp chamois.

Into the garbage
Pour a little household ammonia into a plastic trash bag to keep animals from feasting on and making a mess of your garbage.

Shoes as toys?
Never use an old shoe as a dog toy. He'll think all shoes are made for him and there go your Guccis.

In the dog house
Use a wooden barrel on its side as a dog house. A concrete block on each side will anchor it in place.

A scrap of indoor-outdoor carpeting makes a good flap for the entry to a dog house.

Cedar shavings help the doghouse smell better and thus Rover does, too.

If you live in cotton-growing country, a bed of cotton seeds make for a warmer dog house.

A hot dog idea

Use a bare bulb ceramic socket, a one-pound coffee can, a two-pound can, and their lids. Punch holes all over the sides of the cans. Mount the socket with a forty-watt bulb on a board with the lids sandwiched between them, the smaller lid next to the socket. With the socket wired in, the cans snap into their lids. The bulb throws off enough heat to take the chill off but the bulb is protected against a bump from the pooch.

Some Catty Remarks

Potted plants aren't potties

Keep Tabby from using your large houseplant as a cat box by planting a few mothballs in the soil.

A cat saver idea

Always check your dryer before tossing the clothes in. We often leave the door open after removing the clothes, and cats find this a nice place for a catnap.

Off the furniture

The same tricks that work for dogs will keep the cats off.

Cover the furniture with a large plastic drop cloth when you're not around. Cats can't get comfortable on the plastic and will soon realize they're not welcome on the couch.

For the Birds

Easier feeding

Rig up your bird feeder on a pulley so you can replenish the food without having to climb a ladder. Then raise up away from the enemy.

Take a bath

If the birds ignore your bird bath, put some colorful glass marbles in the water.

Also, float some seeds on the water.

FUN AND GAMES

Golf

Tee time
Rather than a bunch of loose tees, a three-inch strip of corrugated board will hold tees in the holes in the corrugation.

A protection club
Auto paste wax is good protection for woods and irons.

Plastic bowl covers from the kitchen will cover the wheels on a hand golf cart when placed in the trunk of the car. No mud in the trunk.

Tennis

Life after death
Toss a dead tennis ball in with the laundry and, after washing, into the dryer. It may regain most of its life.

Ping Pong

For the next dents
A ping pong ball that is dented can often be restored by putting it in water and bringing it to a boil for a while.

Camping

Stove in a can
Punch holes around the side and at the bottom of a coffee can and insert a roll of toilet paper soaked in paint thinner or denatured alcohol. You have a camp stove for cooking and warmth. (This fire burns long enough that it could be used in a greenhouse during a power failure.)

An old refrigerator shelf is a good grate to go over a pit for camp cooking.

No broken eggs
When carrying eggs for a campout, bury them in the flour or coffee for protection.

Cooking utensils

Make a camp skillet by pulling the bottom of a wire hanger to form a square. Then use aluminum foil to cover this opening.

A wire-cage-type popcorn popper is good for broiling hot dogs and other camp food.

To cook potatoes in campfire coals, stick several nails through each. The nails are good heat conductors for faster, fuller cooking.

Cleanup time

Clean cookware with white wood ash, hot water, and elbow grease.

Make a dishpan by digging out a spot in the ground and lining it with a plastic trash bag.

A leaking tent

Temporarily patch a leaking tent with rubber cement.

For a more permanent repair, apply an iron-on denim patch and then coat it with a spray-on water-proofer.

Dry matches

Store matches in a 35mm film can to keep them dry.

Or, wrap them tightly in foil.

Dip the heads of matches in linseed oil. When dry, the matches become waterproof.

Melted wax does the same thing.

A faster fire starter

Rubber cement spread on kindling gets the campfire going fast.

A corny idea

Carry along some corn cobs dipped in melted paraffin. They're great fire starters.

Bug bites

Insects don't like to coexist. If you get stung, moisten the spot and sprinkle with meat tenderizer to relieve the pain.

A dry sleeping bag

Rather than put your sleeping bag on damp ground, roll out a couple of strips of aluminum foil for the bag to rest on.

Laundry

With a clean plunger and a bucket, you have a washing machine. Put in the water and detergent, add the clothes, and the plunger becomes a great agitator . . . as long as your arm holds out.

Fishing

Opening a can of worms

If you use worms, you know they head for the bottom of the container. Cut out both top and bottom of a two-pound coffee can and put a plastic lid on each end. Just flip the can and all the worms are at the top.

Pour beet juice in the worm can and the slimys will develop a reddish color that is most attractive to fish.

Bubble gum rolled out to resemble a worm may catch some big ones.

Soaked pieces of macaroni may also fool the fish.

Keep plastic worms stored in a jar of water to prevent melting.

Other bait

After driving to your favorite fishing hole, check the radiator. You'll usually find a couple of big grasshoppers to use for bait.

Sock away your reel

Store your reel in an old sweat sock.

Where's that license?

Roll up your fishing license and keep it in a plastic toothbrush holder. It's watertight and will fit easily in the tackle box.

Or, roll it and keep it in an empty fountain pen case or ball point pen barrel. Now you can clip it onto your shirt pocket.

A good hold-up

Use sections of PVC pipe to stick in the beach or shore to act as pole holders.

"X" marks the spot

Mark a good fishing spot with a capped plastic jug connected to a weight by a rope.

Don't get hooked

Store hooks with the points between strips of masking tape, sticky sides face to face. Protects you and the hooks.

Anytime the hook is out of water, crumple a small piece of aluminum foil around the hook. There's less likelihood of anyone getting hooked because the hook is covered and because it's easily seen.

Tilt the scales

Make a fish scaler from bottle caps nailed to a stick, rough side out.

Boating

Waterproof your valuables

A coffee can with a snap-on lid will keep your watch, billfold, and other goodies dry and will float if your boat turns over.

The unsinkable key

Keep your boat key tied to a cork so if dropped, it floats.

Trailer tricks

If you park your boat and trailer at home, even though it's locked, it may be easily stolen. Take one of the wheels off the trailer and it becomes hard to haul away.

You wouldn't think of leaving on a trip without a spare for the car . . . but how about one for your boat trailer?

Bailout

When bailing water out, flatten one side of a can for faster pick-up. This allows the can to get more water with each scoop.

Bicycling

Hang it all

A bike will take up less room in the garage if hung from a large hook in the ceiling.

Rack 'em up
Make a rack to hold all the family bikes by getting an iron bed headboard that has a series of vertical posts. Set it in concrete so that the bottom rail is against the ground. The bike's front wheel goes in between posts and the bike stands in place.

The Hobby Shop

A tray trick
Use a TV tray for all your small projects. It's the right height and parts can't easily roll off. When you take a break, slide the tray out of the way.

WINTER WONDERLAND

Snow Shovels

Digging out
Heat the snow shovel and rub candle wax over it. The snow won't stick to the tool.

Use a dustpan for removing snow from window ledges. The short handle is very convenient.

Or, a child's broom may do the job.

Freeze warning
Test all outside water shutoffs in the fall before winter is here.

Slippery steps
Enlarge the holes in a sprinkler can and use it to sprinkle sand over icy steps.

Or, use the fertilizer spreader for this.

Clean your feet
An old push broom can be attached to the back step to brush snow off of shoes.

MERRY CHRISTMAS

The Christmas Tree

Picking a fresh one

A dry tree is a fire hazard. Here are some ways to pick a fresh one:

- Stick your nose against the tree. It should have a strong aroma.
- Scratch the trunk with your thumb nail. The fresh tree will be juicy under the bark.
- Flex small branches. If they break, the tree is too dry.
- Or, rap the trunk down hard against the ground. A shower of needles means you should move on.

Keeping it fresh

When you get your tree home, cut off a half inch from the bottom of the trunk to remove the caked-over end. Then keep the end in water until it's time to bring it in.

Drill a hole up into the center of the trunk and stuff it with cotton. This acts as wick so the tree drinks more.

If you get tree sap on your hands, rub them with mayonnaise and then wipe away with a paper towel.

Here's a magic formula to keep the tree fresh:

1 gallon warm water
4 tablespoons of horticulture iron powder
4 teaspoons of liquid laundry bleach
2 cups of Karo crystal clear corn syrup

Pour this mix into the tree stand. If there's any left over, use it to replace what the tree drinks the next day. After that, use warm water to keep the stand filled. (Be sure to keep electrical cords away from the tree stand.)

Artificial trees

As you assemble, coat the ends of the branches with petroleum jelly for faster assembly and easier removal after the holidays.

Lights

The tangled web

If you have several strings in a giant snarl, plug in one set and the untangling will be easier.

Ornaments and Decorating

Making ornaments
Make dazzling tree hangers from mirror scraps. Cut matching rectangles and glue them together after slipping a loop of green thread between the pieces. The mirrors will reflect the tree lights.

A good hang up
Dye pipe cleaners green to use for hanging lights and other tree things.

Another hang-up
Hang a wreath on a steel entry door using magnet.

After Christmas storage
Egg cartons will safeguard Christmas balls in storage.

Store larger ornaments in the compartments of a wine bottle carton.

The long tubes from wrapping paper will house a string of lights.

An old sweat sock can protect large balls. Use rubber bands between balls to keep them apart.

The tree must go
Rather than leave a trail of needles throughout the house, use pruning shears to clip off branches and poke them in trash bags. When you're down to the bare trunk, haul the bags out to the compost heap.

If the tree still looks fairly good, remove the decorations and move the tree outside. Redecorate with bread, berries, and other goodies that birds like and both you and the birds with enjoy it a little longer.

Going Places

THE FAMILY CAR

Washing and Cleaning

Mix it yourself
Make your own car washing solution with two cups of kerosene mixed into a gallon of hot water. Sponge it on and rinse it off. This takes off even the worst road grime and leaves a thin film that lets water just bead up.

Free scrubbers
Soft carpet scraps make good car scrubbers.
    It's not free, but a dust mop cover makes a great scrubber. Your hand fits into the pocket.

Bugs
Nylon net will remove insects and other debris without scratching.
    A damp sponge dipped in baking soda also removes insects safely.

Tea time
Use leftover tea to clean the windshield and headlights.

Upholstery cleaning
The foaming bathroom cleaner also cleans vinyl upholstery.
    Try stale beer on leather upholstery. Apply with a clean rag and wipe it off with a damp sponge.

White sidewalls
A soaped steel wool dish pad makes quick work of cleaning white sidewall tires.

Floor mats
Toss the mats into the washer and let several bath towels do the scrubbing for you.

Chrome
A crumpled wad of aluminum foil will clean and shine the bumper. This trick won't clean, but dry flour rubbed with a dry cloth on dry chrome will make it gleam.

If you have wire wheels, use a baby bottle brush to get into the hard-to-reach places.

This tool also works on the grill, as does a vegetable brush.

The chamois
To renew a stiff chamois, soak for fifteen minutes in a gallon of warm water to which a teaspoon of olive oil has been added.

Or, soak in this solution: a tablespoon of glycerin in a half gallon of warm water.

A quick dry
Why not use your leaf blower for quick drying after washing the car.

A quickie bath
For a quick sponge bath, use a wet sponge followed by a rub down with a chamois.

Wiper ways
If the driver-side wiper isn't doing very well and the passenger blade is better, make a swap until new blades can be put on.

Sometimes you can revive blades by using sandpaper all along the edge.

Keep the best of the two wiper blades at replacement time. It will make quick work of removing dew from the side windows.

That extra blade will also remove the fog inside car windows.

The wax works
For a great car wax applicator, put two tablespoons of wax into an old sweat sock. Keep it stored in a sealed glass jar. Warm with a hair dryer if the wax is too hard. The heat from rubbing will keep it soft.

Use cornstarch on a rag to get an even better shine after waxing.

Tar spots
Coat tar spots with linseed oil. Wait an hour and they easily wipe away.

Maintenance Magic

Don't weight for better mileage
Do you still have that hundred pound sack of cement in the trunk of your car? You should know that extra weight will cut back your mileage at a rate of about two percent per hundred pounds. With some of us, that's an incentive to go on a diet.

A quart low?
Make the dipstick easier to read by drilling tiny holes at the "full" and "add" lines.

When changing oil filters, slip a plastic bag over the old one. The wrench will still grip the filter through the bag and when it comes loose, the bag catches all the oil.

When draining the oil, line the pan under the car with a plastic bag and the container never gets oily.

Give your filter wrench a better grip by gluing a strip of sandpaper along the inside gripping surface.

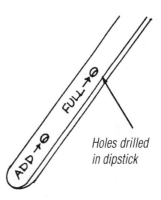

Holes drilled in dipstick

The plastic lid from a one-pound coffee can will also seal a quart motor oil can.

Or, punch two nail holes in the lid, and then let the nail heads plug up the holes and protect the leftover oil from airborne dust.

Store a punch-type oil spout in a plastic bag to catch the drips.

Screaming Belts?
Rub a bar of soap over a slipping belt to stop the squealing.

Hoses
When working with a radiator hose, soak it in hot water for a few minutes to make it more flexible and easier to work with.

Headlights

Just after having your headlights aligned, come home and draw the outline made by the lights, on both high and low on the end wall of the garage. Also mark the distance the car is from the wall. Check from time to time to see that the lights are still okay.

Battery

A light coat of petroleum jelly over battery posts and cable ends retards acid buildup.

Air filter

To see if the air filter is dirty, put a hang light in the opening.

Light shows dirt.

AM/FM

Keep the antenna moving with ease by occasionally lubricating it with a piece of wax paper.

Working under the car

You know that when you look up, a piece of grit will fall in your eye. Not if you wear goggles or even a swim mask.

The flashlight will stay in place aimed up if you put it in a glass jar when working under the car.

Under the hood

When leaning over, make sure your belt buckle doesn't scratch the car finish. An old bathmat or towel will protect the finish.

Form a shield with foil to keep the glare of a drop light from getting in your eyes.

Slit tennis ball covers trailer hitch.

Protection until you get hitched

If you have a trailer hitch, keep it covered with a slit tennis ball until you need to use it again. Before you slip the cover on, coat the hitch with petroleum jelly or a light grease.

Roadside Repairs

Out of gas? 6

Never carry a can of gasoline in your trunk. If you were rear-ended it could explode. However, it's a good idea to have an *empty* can . . . just in case.

If the spout doesn't quite reach into the tank or if you have to carry gas in a spoutless can, make a funnel out of the road map. It will last longer than you think.

Or, roll up a vinyl floor mat.

A large manila envelope can be a onetime funnel. Just make a cut diagonally across the envelope and then a small hole at the corner for the gas to come out.

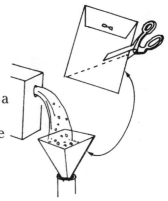

Glue a magnet to your gas cap so it can stay in place right next to the opening. That way you can't ignore it.

Or, paint the dipstick, oil filler cap, and gas cap a bright color so you can't ignore them after checking and adding fluids.

When you notice that gas gauge showing low, use a clothespin attached to the turn-indicator handle to remind you to stop for a fill-up. Paint it a bright color or write "GAS" so you can't ignore it.

No drips

Chewing gum can be put over a gas tank leak as a temporary patch. It'll hold long enough to make it in for repairs.

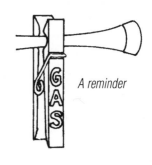

A reminder

Another temporary tank patch is to rub a bar of soap back and forth over the hole.

Keeping clean

Install a paper towel rack in the trunk on the underside of the deck to clean up after road repair.

A pair of those throw-away coveralls are a good thing to have.

Maybe you like the idea of an old window shade in the trunk. When you're going to have to get on the ground, roll out the shade and stay cleaner.

Tire trouble

If you're not into lifting a heavy spare, keep a flat shovel in the trunk. After wrestling the spare out of the trunk, slide the shovel under the tire and use foot pressure on the handle to raise the spare so it can be positioned on the lug posts.

Slip a section of garden hose over the jack handle for a better grip plus protection against a slip that could damage the car.

Mark lines on the jack so you'll know when the car is high enough. That way you won't have to pump it a few more times when you try to put the full spare back on. Front and back can be at different levels.

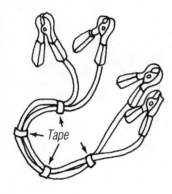

Jump start

So that jumper cables don't get all tangled, lay them out side by side and tape them together in two or three places.

Fuses

If a blown fuse leaves you without lights, wrap the fuse in foil to get back to safety. Be sure to replace it as soon as possible.

The fender bender

A bent fender that rubs the tire can often be moved enough for driving with the bumper jack.

Try using the suction from a plumber's friend to pop out a door dent.

Safety

Protection against hot engine parts

A barbecue mitt is a handy way to reach into a hot engine without burning your fingers.

Be more visible on the road side

Reflective tape may make your car safer in case of problems. Put strips along the inside door facing the driver's side. Headlights from a car coming from behind will pick up the fact that you're getting out.

Also put strips inside the trunk lid.

Keys and Locks

Frozen locks

If the door or trunk lock is frozen you can usually thaw it out if you'll just hold the key over the flame from a lighter for a few moments. You may have to reheat but eventually you're in.

Or, sometimes you can cup your hands around the lock and let your hot breath do the job.

Prevent lock freeze-up by keeping the lock lubricated with a squirt of spray lubricant or cigarette lighter fluid.

Or, put a small patch of waterproof tape over the opening. Keep out moisture and there's nothing to freeze.

Year 'round lock care
Squirt rubbing alcohol followed by a couple puffs of graphite powder. The alcohol carries the powder all through the lock and evaporates, leaving only the lubricant.

The extra key
You can hide a car key under the license plate. Remove the screws and reinstall with the key behind the plate.

TRIP TIPS

An Emergency Kit

Just in case
Be sure you have a spare tire, a jack, a lug wrench, a flashlight, jumper cables, emergency flares, spare fuses, a fan belt, duct tape, an adjustable wrench, a set of screwdrivers, work gloves, a utility knife, a siphon hose, an empty gas can, and a quart of oil.

Security While You're Away

Make it look lived in
Have a neighbor pick up the mail and newspaper each day.

If possible, get someone to park a car in the front drive.

Use timers to turn lights off and on at various times. Do the same for the radio.

Keep the lawn mowed and hedges trimmed.

Get a neighbor to add some of his garbage to your trash bin.

Maps

Before you leave
Get all the maps before you leave and use a marker to highlight the route. Cut out the parts of the map where you'll be traveling and number them in sequence. Use a rubber band to hold the one you're currently using onto the visor.

Strange Service Stations

Not all are friendly
Stay with your car at all times when an attendant is checking tires, under the hood, or running your credit card through the machine.

Lights

Gift wrap the headlights
Before dark, cover the headlights with plastic wrap. When they get too covered with bugs and road film, peel off the wrap and the lights will again do their job.

Invest in a cleaner rearview mirror
Between service stations, you can easily clean your rearview mirror. Just wad up a dollar bill and it'll give you a clearer view behind. Don't throw away the cleaner. It's still spendable.

MOVING DAY

Packing

Zip open boxes
Lay a piece of kite string down where the tape goes on a packed box, with a few inches sticking out on each end. When you get there, pull the string and it will zip open the tape.

No tape licking
Wet the wrapping tape with a cut potato.When the spud begins to get dry, dip it in water.

Different containers
Pack blankets and clothes in plastic trash bags.

Plastic garbage cans are strong and lightweight containers for things to be moved.

Protection and padding
Towels, washcloths, and other small linens can be used as packing material for breakables.

Popcorn is a good protective packing material and you can snack as you unpack.

Disposable diapers are good protective packing.

Tape a frame with glass facing toward the underside of a card table.

A guide for the movers

Color code or otherwise mark all items to indicate which room in the new house each item goes. Include a map.

Carry-ons

Set aside a survival package of stuff you'll need before the movers get there. Include toilet paper, soap, towels, cleansing powder, paper towels, instant coffee, cups, spoons, light bulbs, a can opener, and a first aid kit.

Also, take enough clothes for several days. The van sometimes doesn't get there as quickly as you do.

The refrigerator

Put several charcoal briquettes in each compartment of the refrigerator and freezer to absorb odors.

Or, put a cut loaf of bread in to absorb during the trip.

If the refrigerator has been shipped lying down, don't plug it in until it's been upright for at least twenty-four hours.

Last Minute Checklist

Services to be discontinued

Have all utilities discontinued and don't forget to ask for a deposit refund.

Don't forget cable TV plus any regular service such as milk delivery, newspapers, or pest control.

If you want your bills forwarded, fill out the proper cards at the post office.

Did you forget?

Have you got anything in layaway, items in for repair, clothing left to be cleaned, or a mink coat in storage?

When You Arrive

Bombs away

If you have a spare day before the family actually moves in, set off bug bombs throughout the house. Even if you don't see 'em, they're probably there.

Odds and Ends

HANDY MATH CALCULATIONS

How High?

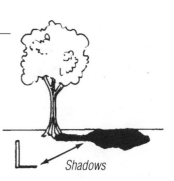

Shadows

The shadow knows
If you wish to know how tall a tree or flag pole is, pick a time of day when the sun is making the object cast a shadow. Put a stick in the ground to also cast a shadow. The length of the shadows is in direct proportion to the length of the object casting it. A little math will tell you the height of the taller object.

Not just a lot of hot air
Use a helium-filled balloon on a long string. When the balloon is even with the top of the object, haul it back in and measure the string.

Roofing

How many shingles?
Shingles are figured in terms of squares. A square is one hundred square feet.

   Because the roof is sloped, you can't just measure the ground area. However, measure the ground area and establish the pitch of the roof and your roofing supply dealer will have a chart with the multiplying factors to let you know how many squares you need.

Concrete

How many yards?
Concrete is measured by volume, usually by cubic

yards. However, most homeowner projects are better understood by thinking in terms of cubic feet. To find the volume of a project, multiply length times width times thickness and divide by twelve. There are twenty-seven cubic feet in a yard.

How many yards in a bag?
An eighty-pound bag of pre-mixed concrete will yield two-thirds or 0.66 of a cubic foot. It would take slightly over forty sacks to make a cubic yard.

Bricks

How many bricks?
The width of the mortar joints has a big effect on the number of bricks required.

For example, a one-fourth-inch joint would require seven bricks per square foot. With a three-eighths-inch joint, only 6.55 bricks. Doesn't sound like much, but when you've got a big project it adds up.

What's the yield of a bag of mortar?
The eighty-pound bag of mortar mix will lay sixty-five bricks or twenty-seven standard concrete blocks using a three-eighths-inch joint.

Board Feet

Wooden shoes?
A board foot is the equivalent of a board that is one foot long and one foot wide and an inch thick. That means that a 2x4 would have to be eighteen inches long to be a board foot. But, that refers to *nominal* size, before the lumber is run through the mill. The *actual* size of a 1x12 board would be three quarters of an inch thick by eleven and one-fourth inches. But it still measures twelve inches in length.

Confused?
Don't worry, lumber is sold by the linear foot at places where do-it-yourselfers do most of their buying.

The Perfect Angle

Right on!

Even without a square, you can establish the perfect right angle, if you can remember 3:4:5. Start with a stake where you want the right angle. Come out with a string three feet in one direction and four feet in another, making it look like a right angle. Form a triangle and, when you adjust to make the third leg exactly five feet, you have the perfect ninety-degree angle.

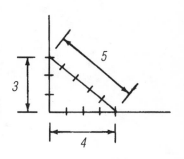

Good Shapes

Round and round we go

No compass to draw a circle? Put a tack through the hole in a hacksaw blade and put a pencil between two teeth. The teeth keep the pencil at the proper distance as you swing the blade around for a perfect circle.

It's elliptical

A pair of tacks, a loop of string, and a pencil is all you need to draw an ellipse. With the tacks a few inches apart and the loop around them, use the pencil to pull the string taut to form a triangle. Now, as you keep the string taut, move the pencil around the tacks and, when you get back to the starting point, you'll have an ellipse. Adjust the spacing of the tacks and the size of the loop to adjust the size of the ellipse.

NEW USES
FOR OLD STUFF

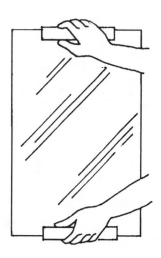

Garden Hose

Hand saver

A couple of slit sections of hose slipped over the edges of a pane of glass will let you carry it without slicing your hands.

Rope saver

Slip a section of hose over a rope that may rub against something.

Energy saver
Staple a hose section to the garage door bottom as a weatherstrip. An even better one is a worn out hose from the fire department.

Kid saver
A section of hose stapled to the edges of a kid's swing can cushion against injury.

Plastic Jugs

Cutting remarks
First, here's a tip on cutting plastic containers. Fill the jug with hot water and let it sit for several minutes. When you drain the water, the materials will be easier to cut and more flexible. Tin snips or large scissors work well. Where holes are needed, use an icepick.

A free funnel
The tops of many jugs can become funnels if you cut off the bottom.

Here's the scoop
Make a scoop by cutting away the bottom with a diagonal cut from just below the handle to just above the bottom.

Need a bucket?
Add a rope handle to the bottom half of a large jug and you've got a bucket.

A clothespin caddy
Cut a hole in a plastic jug from just under the spout to about midway. Then remove the bottom one-third of the handle. You have a clothespin holder that hangs from the line. You may also want to drill a few holes in the bottom to let rain water drain out.

A boat saver
Flat jugs are good bumpers for boats and boat docks.

Fooling with Jack Frost
Jugs filled with sand can be kept in the trunk for tire traction on slick and icy spots.

Yea, team!
Cut away the bottom of a large jug and you have a megaphone.

More Plastics

Not such a pill
Pill bottles can hold all sorts of tiny parts and you can see the contents.

Inner Tubes

Where are they?
With nothing but tubeless tires, many folks think there aren't that many inner tubes. Ask at your service station and, if they do any tire repair business, they'll usually have a few old inner tubes around.

Silence the chains
Store your tire chains in a sleeve made from an inner tube. Tape one end and use rubber bands to close the other. No rattling noise!

Six-pack Plastic Loops

A handy tote
Remove the tops from the cans and put them back in the rings. Now you have a tote for six different sizes of nails.

How does your hammer hang?
Cut the loops into two pieces with three holes each. Loop one over your belt in a slip knot and the loop that hangs down holds a hammer at your side. Loop it over a ladder rung and the hammer can be held there for work up high.

Carpeting

Foot saver
A strip of carpet in front of the workbench will be kinder to the feet.

A plush bench top
Carpet the top of the workbench to protect fine work and prevent things from rolling off.

In the car
Cover the inside of the car trunk and be kind to your luggage.

No more door dinks
Attach a square on the garage wall to protect the open car door.

Perk up the pickup
Indoor-outdoor carpet makes a good cover for the pickup bed.

Old Tires

Pick up on this
Small items in the back of a pickup truck will be fenced in by a tire and can't roll around.

Parquet Flooring

Table this one
Use the squares to cover a coffee or end table.

A-door-able
Line up squares at the bottom of a door to act as a kickplate.

Wallpaper

The mellow pages
Cover the phone book with wallpaper.

Nothing trashy here
Apply paper over a waste basket.

Something's in the air
Make a pattern and cover the blades of a ceiling fan.

Motor Oil

A slick trick
Brush the oil on snow shovels and the snow doesn't stick. It also helps the snow blower.

Free of rust . . . for free
Use it to coat anything metal to prevent rust.

Air-sickness Bags

While you're waiting
You'll probably come up with other new uses for drained motor oil. Until you do, store it in an air-sickness bag from your last flight.

Newspapers

Save 'em
For easier bundling, there is one size grocery sack just right for sliding in sections of newspaper. When full, tie it up.

Besides training your puppy and lining the bird-cage, here are some more uses:

Free heat
Tightly rolled sections can be banded with wire and used as fireplace logs.

Packing
Shred or wad to serve as packing material around breakables.

Insulate
Newspaper is good insulation for keeping ice cream frozen longer.

Dry feet
A wad crammed into wet boots and shoes absorbs moisture and helps footware keep its shape.

Paint drips
Use as a substitute drop cloth for painting.

Free money
If you have any left after all these new uses, bundle 'em and take them to a recycling center. . .often for cash.

Toothbrushes

The brush off
Because of the size, a toothbrush is great for cleaning small parts in the shop or garage, for getting down into carvy places in furniture stripping, for getting grime from around faucets, and for cleaning typewriter keys and many other things.

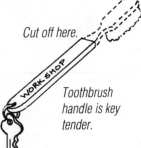

Cut off here.

Toothbrush handle is key tender.

Handle this
Cut off the brush and, if the handle has a hole in it, you've got a dandy key holder for gates and locks.

Keys

Wedged in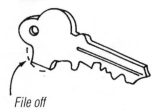
Use your bench grinder to convert keys into metal wedges for securing new wooden tool handles.

File off

In the pocket
Grind the end of an old key to form a screwdriver blade. You'll find many uses for the pocket screwdriver on your key chain.

Anti-freeze

Beware
Whatever you do, you should know that this stuff is attractive to kids and pets and is very poisonous.

Brush cleaner
Drained anti-freeze is a great brush-soaking solvent.

Sandpaper

True grit
Palm a piece of sandpaper to get a better grip on a balky jar lid.

Non-slip slippers
Scuff sand the soles of new shoes to prevent slipping.

A sharp idea
Run a sewing machine needle through sandpaper to sharpen it.

Broom

Sweep in with this one
Trim both the bristles and the handle and you have a large whisk broom.

Blue Jeans

Sandbags
Cut off the legs, sew up the end, fill it with sand, and, when you sew up the other end, you've got a handy sandbag.

Make a shop apron as shown.

Slit a jeans leg longways and stitch across to form pockets. Now you have a hang-up pouch that will hold a variety of things.

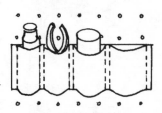

Picket Fencing

Pants leg of denim jeans

Laundry day
A section of fencing placed under the clothes lines will be a platform to keep you from standing in the mud.

Walking the fence
Trim both ends of the pickets on the outside of the twisted wire parts that hold the fence together. Place this flat on the ground and you can make a good walkway.

Mail Box

Special delivery
Mount one of those rural-type mailboxes on the fence in your garden. It will hold hand tools and gloves and keep 'em handy and dry.

Golf Tees

Wedge-wood
Cut off one side of a tee so it's flat and you have a wedge for many purposes.

Paint Buckets

Free pail
Wash out an empty latex paint bucket before the paint sets up. Remove the rim with a can opener and you have a handy pail.

PVC Plastic Drain Pipe

Plastic drain pipe

Nothing to wine about
Use several foot-long sections glued together to make a wine rack that hangs from a refrigerator shelf.

Or, use several stacked and glued together as a countertop wine rack.

A plumb clever idea
Cluster several different short lengths of PVC with end caps and when you glue them together you have a desk set to hold pencils, pens, and other such things.

Electrical Wire

Tie one on
The two strands in lamp cord easily pull apart, and the single wire is great as a heavy duty twist tie for trash bags.

It's also good for tying bundles.

Rubber Gloves

Strike up the band
Use scissors to cut gloves into jillions of rubber bands of various sizes. Even use the fingers for tiny rubber bands.

Old Scissors

Cut out and save
An old pair of scissors with a broken blade can become a neat pair of tin snips by just grinding off the other blade and then rounding both. You might want to sharpen them, too.

Canteen

Drink in this idea
An old army canteen makes a unique hanging planter for ivy.

Nose Drops Bottles

Nothing to sniffle at
Fill with oil and use the dropper to get the oil in place.

Plastic Shower Curtains

Gotcha covered
Save as a drop cloth for painting.

During the off-season, cover the outside part of a room air conditioner with the curtain, using duct tape to hold it in place. Keeps cold air from getting in.

A shower curtain is also good as a tarp for covering all sorts of things outside.

Shower Curtain Rings

Just hanging out
Metal rings will hold all sorts of small items like washers,

Shower curtain ring

nuts, and the like so these parts can be hung from a hook where they're much easier to spot.

Hang one from a belt loop and it will hold your hammer.

Dental Tools

Open wide
After use, some tools may not still be good for use by the dentist. However, you'll find his pliers, scrapers, picks, and mirrors to be of help for many projects
around the home and shop. Ask your dentist to save them for you.

SHOW US YOUR BEST
HANDY HINTS

If you've enjoyed this collection of handy hints and tips, maybe you've been reminded of a favorite trick of your own that we've missed. If so, why not jot it down and send it for our next hints book? While we won't send you big bucks for your ideas, you'll receive something much greater than money . . . you'll have the reward of knowing that you've helped others.

Send tips to:
Al Carrell
The Super Handyman
P. O. Box 12623
Dallas, TX 75225

Index